THE LIFE OF OUR LORD

AN ENDURING LEGACY OF CHRISTIAN FAITH

THE LIFE OF OUR LORD

AN ENDURING LEGACY OF CHRISTIAN FAITH

Compilation and Biography by Gene Fedele

CHARLES DICKENS

Newberry, FL 32669

Bridge-Logos
Newberry, FL 32669

**The Life of Our Lord:
An Enduring Legacy of Christian Faith**
by Charles Dickens
Compilation and Biography by Gene Fedele

Copyright © 2021 by Bridge-Logos

All rights reserved. Under International Copyright Law, no part of this publication may be reproduced, stored, or transmitted by any means—electronic, mechanical, photographic (photocopy), recording, or otherwise—without written permission from the publisher.

Library of Congress Catalog Card Number: 2020949845

International Standard Book Number: 978-1-61036-257-3

eBook International Standard Book Number: 978-0-7684-5947-0

Hardcover International Standard Book Number: 978-0-7684-5998-2

Large Print International Standard Book Number: 978-0-7684-5999-9

Editing services: ChristianEditingServices.com

Cover/Interior design: Kent Jensen | knail.com

Biblical Engravings: Gustave Doré, *The Doré Gallery of Bible Illustrations*

Bible quotations are derived primarily from the King James Version.

CONTENTS

Editor's Dedication vi
Editor's Preface vii
Foreword xi
Biography of Charles Dickens. 1
The Major Works of Charles Dickens. 33

The Life of Our Lord by Charles Dickens 35
Chapter the First. 37
Chapter the Second. 41
Chapter the Third. 47
Chapter the Fourth. 53
Chapter the Fifth 59
Chapter the Sixth 65
Chapter the Seventh. 71
Chapter the Eighth 81
Chapter the Ninth. 87
Chapter the Tenth 91
Chapter the Eleventh 97

Two Prayers written by Charles Dickens
    for His Young Children. 108
Editor Biography. 110

EDITOR'S DEDICATION

In honor of Charles Dickens' motivation for writing *The Life of Our Lord* for his children, I humbly dedicate this edition to my children: Lauren, Christopher (in glory), Caroline, and Rebekah; as well as my grand-daughters: Cézanne, Emma, Avery, and Penny.

EDITOR'S PREFACE

The literary works of Charles Dickens are so well known that few and far between are those who are not at least mildly familiar with his name and writings. He was an English author and universally renowned as one of the world's most prominent novelists of the Victorian era. So many of the characters within his stories have been beloved by adults and children alike. Yet, relatively few are aware of this wonderful book he wrote in 1849, *The Life of Our Lord*, which has not been included in the various collections of his writings that have been published during the past three centuries. In fact, it wasn't until 1934 that it was first permitted publication, by his family, nearly sixty-four years after his death.

The Life of Our Lord is a unique and special book in that it, more than any other, reflects Dickens' love of God and faith in Jesus Christ. Within its pages, the great novelist unfolds the Gospel message of Jesus Christ, hand-written in the beautiful "Dickensian" prose the world has come to adore, specifically for his own children during their earlier years. During his life, he was a man of impeccable reservation and privacy, and had requested of the family that this work remain secluded from the world and sacred within the familial boundaries.

In addition, we see glimpses of Dickens' central theme of many of his novels—compassion for and caring of the poor and needy, based on the biblical principles he cherished—within the story lines of *The Life of Our Lord.* In his introduction of Christ's apostles he records the following instruction for his children: "Heaven was made for them [the poor] as well as for the rich, and that God makes no difference between those who wear good clothes and those who go barefoot and in rags. The most miserable, the most ugly, deformed, wretched creatures that live, will be bright Angels in Heaven if they are good here on earth. Never forget this, when you are grown up. Never be proud or unkind, my dears, to any poor man, woman, or child. If they are bad, think that they would have been better if they had kind friends, and good homes, and had been better taught. So, always try to make them better by kind, persuading words; and always try to teach them and relieve them if you can. And when people speak ill of the poor and miserable, think how Jesus Christ went among them, and taught them, and thought them worthy of His care. And always pity them yourselves, and think as well of them as you can."

Further evidence of this eminent author's Christian faith and passion for truth and justice for the less privileged is reflected in the biography I have written which is largely gleaned from several reliable sources, primarily the first edition of the Life of Charles Dickens, written by his dear friend, R. Shelton MacKenzie, just a few short months after Dickens' death in 1870.

This biographical sketch is not intended as a detailed chronology of the author's life and writings, but instead is primarily a reflection on the heart of the man and the primary motivation behind his great literary works—his faith in Christ and his love for his fellow man.

With humility and adoration, we add this precious book to the distinguished Pure Gold Classics collection in anticipation and expectation that young and old alike will be richly blessed by the simplicity and warmth of the story of the life of our Savior that Dickens left as a blessing to the world and a glorious testimony of his own personal relationship with the Lord.

Editor, Gene Fedele
April 2021

FOREWORD

(Largely compiled by Lady Marie Dickens, from the First English Edition, 1934. Also includes excerpts from the 1939 American edition, and other family notes.)

This book, the last work of Charles Dickens to be published, has an individual interest and purpose that separates it completely from everything else that Dickens wrote.

Quite distinct from its Divine Subject, the words are peculiarly personal to the novelist, and is not so much a revelation of his mind as a tribute to his heart and humanity—and also, of course, his deep devotion to our Lord.

Dickens began writing *The Life of Our Lord* in 1846 and completed it in 1849, twenty-one years before his death, expressly for his children. The simple manuscript is entirely handwritten, and is in no sense a fair copy but a spontaneous draft. Charles Dickens frequently told his children the Gospel Story, and made mention of the Divine Example in his letters to them. This *The Life of Our Lord* was written without thought of publication, in order that his family might have a permanent record of their father's thoughts. The reasons which compelled him to write this simple account of the life of Jesus, and to withhold it from the reading public, are best given in his own words.

A few hours before he was stricken with the attack which caused his death a day later, Dickens wrote a letter to John M. Makeham, who had accused him of irreverence in a passage of *The Mystery of Edwin Drood*. The final paragraph of that letter, perhaps the last words written by Dickens, contained this statement:

> "I have always striven in my writings to express veneration for the life and lessons of Our Saviour, because I feel it; and because I rewrote that history for my children every one of whom knew it from having it repeated to them long before they could read, and almost as soon as they could speak. But I have never made proclamation of this from the housetops."

Part of the manuscript was written in Switzerland. On June 28, 1846, he wrote from Lausanne to Mamie Dickens: "Half of the children's New Testament to write, or pretty nearly. I set to work and did that."

In 1868, when his youngest son, Edward, went to Australia to join an elder brother, Charles Dickens wrote him as follows:

> "I put a New Testament among your books for the very same reason, and with the same hopes, that made me write an easy account of it for you when you were a little child. Because it is the best book that ever was or will be known in the world."

FOREWORD

During his lifetime Charles Dickens refused to permit publication of *The Life of Our Lord* because he doubtless felt that it was a personal letter to his own children, and feared that a public disclosure of so intimate a document might involve the possibility of attack and defense of his deepest religious convictions.

In a letter to a clergyman he said: "There cannot be many men, I believe, who have a more humble veneration for the New Testament, or a more profound conviction of its all-sufficiency than I have. My observation of life induces me to hold in unspeakable dread and horror these unseemly squabbles about 'the letter' which drive 'the Spirit' out of hundreds of thousands."

His wife's sister, Georgina Hogarth, in a letter to Mrs. James T. Fields, has thus recorded the attitude of Charles Dickens toward *The Life of Our Lord*: "I must now tell you about the beautiful little New Testament which he wrote for his children. I am sorry to say it is never to be published. ... He wrote it years ago, when his elder children were quite little. It is about sixteen short chapters, chiefly adapted from Luke's Gospel, most beautiful, most touching, most simple as such a narrative should be. He never would have it printed, and I used to read it to the little boys in manuscript before they were old enough to read themselves. ... I asked Charles if he did not think it would be well for him to have it printed, at all events for private circulation, if he would not publish it. He said he would look over the manuscript and take a week or two to consider. At the end of the time he gave it back to me and said he had decided never to publish it, or even to have it privately printed. He said I might make a copy of it for Peggy (Mrs. Dickens) or any one of his children, but for no one else, and he also begged that we would never even hand the manuscript, or a copy of it, to anyone to take out of the house. So there is no doubt about his strong feeling on the subject, and we must obey it. After his death the original manuscript became mine… it was one of his private papers, which were left to me. So I gave it at once to Mamie, who was, I thought, the most natural and proper possessor of it, as being his daughter."

When *The Life of Our Lord* was finished, Dickens had eight children, the oldest, Charles Jr., having been born in 1837, and the youngest, Henry Fielding, born in January 1849. Sydney was two years old, but the others, ranging from twelve to four, were definitely of an articulate and inquisitive age, so to answer their questions about religion and faith, he decided to set down this simple narrative of the life of Christ.

For eighty-five years the resulting manuscript was sacredly guarded as a precious family secret. After Georgina Hogarth died, it fell to Dickens' youngest child, Sir Henry Fielding Dickens, with the admonition that it should not be published while any child of Dickens lived. Just before the 1933 Christmas holidays Sir Henry died in London. In his will he wrote:

> "I give and bequeath to my wife the original manuscript of my father's *Life of Our Lord*, which was bequeathed to my aunt Georgina Hogarth in my father's will, and given by her to me to hold, on the following trusts: 'Being his son, I have felt constrained to act upon my father's expressed desire that it should not be published, but I do not think

it right that I should bind my children by any such view, especially as I can find no specific injunction against such publication. I therefore direct that my wife and my children should consider this question quite unfettered by any view of mine, and if by a majority they decide that the manuscript should not be published, I direct my wife to deposit it with the trustees of the British Museum upon the usual terms, but if they decide by a majority that it should be published, then I direct my wife to sell the same in trust, to divide the net proceeds of such sale among my wife and all my children in equal shares."

Sir Henry's widow and children, through a majority decision, assumed the right to permit its publication, and *The Life of Our Lord*, by Charles Dickens is thus given to the world. It was first published, in serial form, in March 1934.

BIOGRAPHY OF CHARLES DICKENS

By Gene Fedele

Unlike many of his contemporary novelists whose works reflected scenes and insights from the aristocratic life of English society, Charles Dickens chose rather to develop his stories and draw out his characters from the experiences of the lower classes and the contrasting lives that existed between the classes within 18th and 19th-century English culture. His personal faith in Christ had prompted him to a deep sensitivity and passion for the suffering, needy, and poor of English society—whose dire circumstances were inflicted, at times, in the name of religion. Though his honest and moving exposure of English institutions throughout many stories and characters within his books often drew criticism and persecution from the literary, political, and cultural critics of his day, he was truly a champion of the oppressed and our world is a better and brighter place because of timeless classics he has left us.

The motivation central to his purpose and themes in his writing was his faith in Jesus Christ and his desire to convey gospel truths of hope, love, and our Christian responsibilities to our fellow man. His intentions went well beyond mere humanitarian interests, as was the accusation of some critics, but a genuine, passionate concern for the well-being of his fellow man—specifically as it related to the provision and education of the poor, medical care for the needy, and the individual and societal responsibilities towards charity. His novels consistently echo the rich biblical values and truths he possessed in his heart. Dickens' characterizations of his "good people" within his novels exhibit many of the Christ-like qualities he held so dear and desired to convey to his readers.

R. Shelton MacKenzie, in his biography, *The Life of Charles Dickens* (1870), reflects: "The practical spirit he endeavored to inculcate [in his writing] was that of comprehensive Christianity. His personal character was in accordance with his teaching—charitable, kind-hearted, affectionate, temperate in living, ever doing his work as if he felt it a pleasure rather than a labor. There was a daily beauty in his life, in its earnestness, in its simplicity, in its purity, which was an exemplar in itself."

In writing to a close friend, Reverend David Macrae, Dickens reveals his heart and clear purpose of using specific characters to express the values he most closely identified with Christ: "With a deep sense of my great responsibility always upon me when I exercise my art, one of my most constant and most earnest endeavours has been to exhibit in all my good people some faint reflections of the teachings of our great Master."

In *The Religious Sentiments of Charles Dickens*, the author Charles McKenzie remarks: "Charles Dickens taught Christian truth in his novels, and was a Christian teacher. He never professed to be a theological writer, certainly, but wrote mainly to amuse and thought he was doing a very Christian work by so lightening the burden of this toilsome life for so many who would read [his novels]." McKenzie further comments on Dickens' purpose of exposing the religious hypocrisies of his day within his fiction, and providing genuine and divinely inspired solutions for his readers to contemplate; "The unmasking of hypocrisy is not inconsistent with the character of a Christian teacher and reformer, otherwise Jesus Christ himself was neither... It is the legitimate and dutiful province of all Christian teachers to oppose this worst form of enmity to righteousness in distinct and unfailing terms, and such has Charles Dickens, of all men, done. And had he done only this, without regard for genuine Christian character, he would still have rendered a great service to religion; but he has done more! He has shown a high estimation of true religious character in his books and has portrayed countless unmistakable examples of such."

In an early quotation from his own preface to the *Pickwick Papers*, he professes: "Lest there be those who do not perceive the difference between a humble reverence for the truths of Scripture and an audacious and offensive obtrusion of its letter and not its spirit—let them understand it is always the latter and not the former that is satirized [in my fiction]. It is never out of season to protest against that familiarity with sacred things, or against the confounding of Christianity with any class of persons who have just enough religion to make them hate, and not enough to make them love religion."

Later, within the pages of *Nicholas Nickleby* we find the following discourse: "There are some men who, living with the one object of enriching themselves, by whatever means, and be perfectly conscious of the baseness and rascality of the means they use every day towards this end, affect, nevertheless—even to themselves—a high tone of moral rectitude, and shake their heads and sigh over the depravity of the world. Some of the craftiest scoundrels that ever walked this earth, or rather—for walking implies, at least, an erect position and the bearing of a man—that ever crawled and crept through life by its dirtiest and narrowest ways, will gravely jot down in diaries the events of every day, and keep a regular debtor and creditor account with Heaven, which shall always show a floating balance in their own favour. Whether this is a gratuitous part of the falsehood and trickery of such men's lives, or whether they really hope to cheat Heaven itself, and lay up treasure in the next world by the same process which has enabled them to lay up treasure in this [world]—not to question how it is, so it is."

It is common for biographies of eminent authors to boast of an austere lineage and famous ancestors from whom such genius and greatness is derived, but Charles Dickens did not possess such an illustrious ancestry. Instead, he was quite content to draw his nobility directly from the Creator himself.

Charles was born in Portsmouth, England, in 1812, the second child and eldest son of John and Elizabeth Dickens. John worked for the government as a clerk and was entrusted with large sums of money to disperse salaries and wages to those who served during the Great War with France. He was a man of talent and energy and warmly liked wherever he went and with all sorts of company. Elizabeth was a loving wife, devoted to her children, and Charles always treated her with kindness and affection.

BIRTHPLACE OF CHARLES DICKENS, 1 MILE END TERRACE
(1904, *THE LEISURE HOUR*)

As a boy, Charles received a plain education, but was gifted with a delightful imagination and a love for classic stories, such as *Arabian Knights*, DeFoe's *Robinson Crusoe*, and Cervantes's *Knight of LaMancha*. He showed early promise of his creative genius by his love for education, writing and performing some of his own stories and those of other classical writers.

After his father fell on financial hard times, he was thrown into the debtor's prison and Dickens' family was forced to experience the rough life associated with such shame and ruin. Perhaps even the experiences of poor David Copperfield and the misery he endured at Salem House at the brutal hands of

Mr. Creakle, as well as the story of Little Dorrit whose self-sacrificial attending of her father in a similar prison were not unlike those witnessed by young Charles himself, and the source of inspiration for these delightful classics.

CHARLES DICKENS, 1830

At the tender age of sixteen, Charles secured a position as a clerk writer for a legal firm, which led to a post as a private reporter for *The Mirror of Parliament*, at the age of twenty. Through his success and connections he then worked for the *True Sun*, where Mr. Dickens was known as one of their most dedicated, talented and reliable reporters. It was during this employment that he spent considerable time in observation and contemplation of the nooks and alleys, and "inner life" of London, thus leading to his first set of well-known writings, *Sketches of Boz* (an anonymous pen-name adopted by Dickens, which had been his nickname for a younger brother, and known to only a few reporters), subsequently published in the *Old Monthly Magazine* in 1836. The collection included *Sketches from Our Parish, Scenes in London and Vicinity, Characters,* and several *Tales*; which attracted considerable attention. Some accused him of exaggeration and racy humor, but many appreciated the spirit and fidelity conveyed in these sketches of English life and character, so much so that it led to their publication as his first novel, *The Pickwick Papers* in 1837.

CATHERINE, WIFE OF CHARLES DICKENS

DICKENS MARRIES HOGARTH

Charles Dickens married Catherine Hogarth in 1838, daughter of George Hogarth, a Scottish lawyer who had the rare distinction of having been the friend and adviser of two of the greatest writers of prose fiction his native and his adopted land had even produced—Walter Scott and Charles Dickens. Mr. and Mrs. Dickens had enjoyed their early years as husband and wife, and even had opportunity to travel to Scotland and America together. They had ten children together and they were united in their mutual desire to protect their family and home life from the publicity his growing English and American literary celebrity was bringing upon him.

THE DIVINE PURPOSE IN HIS WRITINGS

About this same time he was working on his next two great novels, *Oliver Twist* and *Nicholas Nickleby*, wherein the former Dickens reflects on much of the cruelty and inhumanity inflicted upon orphaned children by the parish work-house system, and in the latter he exposes similar "crimes" associated with the Yorkshire schools. Here we see, in all its splendid candor and honesty, the passionate heart of Dickens purposed to expose systems of abuse upon the helpless and needy within established institutions—some done even in the name of "religion." Though many public journals published stories of liberal education and good treatment of these children, Dickens, upon personal visitations of these facilities and witnessing abuses of body and mind, was moved to write about what none other would have dared to expose in the journals and papers of the day. It was his intention to awaken, in the hearts and minds of his predominantly middle-class readers, the reality of the desperate plight of the poor and suffering amidst their communities. Through the pages of his fiction Dickens' readers are drawn to identify with his characters and have no choice but to consider the failing responsibility of society and the Church to care for the poor.

OLIVER ASKS FOR MORE, *OLIVER TWIST*
(ENGRAVING: GEORGE GRUCKSHANK, 1867)

In his *Life of Charles Dickens*, John Forster says of the essence of *Oliver Twist*, "It is indeed the primary purpose of the tale to show its little hero, jostled as he is in the miserable crowd, preserved everywhere from the vice of its pollution, by an exquisite delicacy of natural sentiment which clings to him under every disadvantage. There is not a more masterly touch in fiction, and it is by such that this delightful fancy is consistently worked out to the last, than Oliver's agony of childish grief on being brought away from the branch-workhouse, the wretched home associated only with suffering and starvation, and with no kind word or look, but containing still his little companions in misery."

In Dickens' own words he reflects, "Mr. Squeers is the representative of a class, and not of an individual. Where imposture, ignorance, and brutal cupidity, are the stock in trade of a small body of men, and one is described by these characteristics, all his fellows will recognize something belonging to themselves, and each will have a misgiving that the portrait is his own." He added the emphatic declaration that "his object in calling public attention to the system would be very imperfectly fulfilled, if he did not state now in his own person, emphatically and earnestly, that Mr. Squeers and his school are faint and feeble pictures of an existing reality, purposely subdued and kept down lest they should be deemed impossible that there are upon record trials at law in which damages have been sought as a poor recompense for lasting agonies and disfigurements inflicted upon children by the treatment of the master in these places, involving such offensive and foul details of neglect, cruelty, and disease, as no writer of fiction would have the boldness to imagine and that, since he has been engaged upon these adventures, he has received from private quarters far beyond the reach of suspicion or distrust, accounts of atrocities, in the perpetration of which upon neglected or repudiated children these schools have been the main instruments, very far exceeding any that appear in these pages."

Dickens, in response to attacks directed against the subject of the book defending his purpose, declaring that he had "tried to do a service to society in depicting a knot of such associates in crime in all their deformity and squalid wretchedness, skulking uneasily through a miserable life to a painful and shameful death." The immoral will always call into question such writing, but the righteous will see the invaluable lessons of what mankind ought to be from the ugliness of what it often is. Continues Forster, "We cannot too often be told that as the pride and grandeur of mere external circumstances is the falsest of earthly things, so the truth of virtue in the heart is the most lovely and lasting. And from the pages of *Oliver Twist* this teaching is once again to be taken by all who look for it there."

In 1842, Charles Dickens traveled to America, delivering eloquent stories and talks before large crowds in several cities during his 4½ months journey. He received warm receptions wherever he went and was hailed in every place. After his trip to Washington where we met with dignitaries in the House and Senate, the honorable B. B. French records, "Dickens, by his modesty, his social powers, and his eloquence, has added to the high esteem in which I was previously induced to hold him. I believe every person present was delighted." And Mr. Keim proposed Mr. Dickens' health in the following exalted terms: "Philanthropy and genius, and a representative of both, now our guest in Washington, whom [George] Washington himself would have rejoiced to welcome."

In 1843, the genius of Charles Dickens reached new heights with the publication of *A Christmas Carol*. Its reception and success was overwhelming. "My purpose," says the author, "was, in a whimsical kind of masque which the good-humor of the season justified, to awaken some loving and fostering thought never out of season in a Christian land." Having struck a fresh vein of greatness, the Lord Jeffrey wrote of Dickens's new tale, "we are all charmed with your *Carol*, chiefly, I think, for the genuine goodness which breathes all through it, and is the true inspiring angel by which its genius has been awakened. The whole scene of the Cratchetts is like the dream of a beneficent angel in spite of its broad reality and little Tiny Tim, in life and death almost as sweet and as touching as Nelly. And then the schoolboy scene, with that large-hearted, delicate sister, with his gall-lacking liver and milk of human-kindness for blood, and yet all so natural and so humbly and serenely happy." How could anyone familiar with this precious "ghost story" fail to rejoice in the impact of a life transformed from one of extreme parsimoniousness and disregard for human suffering into one defined by joy, generosity, and redemption."

MARLEY'S GHOST VISITS SCROOGE. *A CHRISTMAS CAROL*

In this irresistibly warm tale of human transformation Dickens' readers are introduced to several characters that embody the very principles of Christian charity (Bob Cratchett; the three spirits; Old Fezzywig; Scrooge's nephew, Fred; and his sister, Fan), and their selfless, benevolent engagement of those desperately in need of it (Ebenezer Scrooge). *A Christmas Carol*, more than any other of his novels published at this point in Dickens' young literary career, unfolds for his readers the biblical truths of contrasting good and evil, condemnation and redemption, and Judgment and Resurrection.

After a few years rest from his labors and travels, Dickens wrote what he professed to be one of his favorite books, *David Copperfield*, primarily because it was in many ways autobiographical. Yet, it was at this same time that he penned the most personal of his writings, *The Life of Our Lord*. This subject was so dear to him and his desire to share it with his then young children so deeply intimate, that his solemn request to his wife and children was that this book would never be published or placed in the public eye. It wasn't until two generations later and through much deliberation that the family would conclude that this precious book should not be denied the blessing it was destined for in bringing the Gospel message of Jesus Christ to the hearts and lives of so many!

In 1857 Dickens' *Little Dorrit* was completed and published for the world. This latest edition to his works presented to its readers the sharp contrast between the harsh and evil effects of imprisonment for debt, particularly those victimized who are

LITTLE DORRITT

least capable of fulfilling the claims of debtors upon them, and the delightful innocence, devotion, and genuine sacrificial charity of precious Little Dorrit.

DOMESTIC TROUBLES

Difficult family times followed with the emotional illness of his wife, Catherine, which led to a regretful divorce in June of 1858. Dickens was grieved over her condition and the resulting family trauma. He shared his heart in the matter in a letter to his friend, Arthur Smith, May 25, 1858:

> "Mrs. Dickens and I have lived unhappily together for many years. Hardly any one who has known us intimately can fail to have known that we are, in all respects of character and temperament, wonderfully unsuited to each other.

I suppose that no two people, not vicious in themselves, ever were joined together who had a greater difficulty in understanding one another, or who had less in common.

For some years past Mrs. Dickens has been in the habit of representing to me that it would be better for her to go away and live apart; that her always increasing estrangement was due to a mental disorder under which she sometimes labors; more, that she felt herself unfit for the life she had to lead, as my wife, and that she would be better far away. I have uniformly replied that she must bear our misfortune, and fight the fight out to the end; that the children were the first consideration; and that I feared they must bind us together in 'appearance.'

At length, within these three weeks, it was suggested to me by [John] Forster that, even for their sakes, it would surely be better to reconstruct and rearrange their unhappy home." I empowered him to treat with Mrs. Dickens, as the friend of us both. Mrs. Dickens wished to add, on her part, Mark Lemon, and did so. On Saturday last Lemon wrote to Forster that Mrs. Dickens "gratefully and thankfully accepted" the terms I proposed to her...which I believe are as generous as if Mrs. Dickens were a lady of distinction, and I a man of fortune. As for the children—my eldest boy to live with Mrs. Dickens and take care of her; my eldest girl to keep my house, and all the children to live with me in the continued companionship of their Aunt Georgina, for whom they have all the tenderest affection that I have ever seen among young people, and who has a higher acclaim (as

I have often declared, more many years), upon my affection, respect and gratitude than anybody in the world.

SKETCH OF CHARLES DICKENS WITH WIFE, CATHERINE, AND HER SISTER, GEORGINA.

I hope no one who may become acquainted with what I write here, can possibly be so cruel and unjust as to put any misconstruction on our separation. My elder children all understand it perfectly, and all accept it as inevitable. There is not a shadow of doubt or concealment among us.

Two wicked persons, who should have spoken differently of me, in consideration of earnest respect and gratitude, have coupled with the separation the name of a young lady for whom I have great attachment and regard. I will not repeat her name—I honor it too much. Upon my soul and honor, there is not on this earth a more virtuous and spotless creature than that young lady. I know her to be innocent and pure, and as good as my own dear daughters.

Further, I am quite sure that Mrs. Dickens, having received this assurance from me, must now believe it in the respect I know her to have for me, and in the perfect confidence I know her in her better moments to repose in my truthfulness. Again, all this is open between my children and me. They are perfectly certain that I would not deceive them, and the confidence among us is without fear."

Unfortunately, from the time of these events even until modern day, there have been numerous dubious reports maligning the circumstances and motives surrounding Charles Dickens's personal life and particularly those regarding his marriage and subsequent separation from his wife. Such accusations include those of supposed marriage infidelity with one or more persons, conspiring to have his wife committed to an insane asylum, and deceiving the public of these (fallacious) events. Many have been the result of unsubstantiated, fabricated and even malicious information leading to the publication of slanderous articles designed to defame and sensationalize the reputation of such a public figure, while others have been deliberate, even envious, acts of what Dickens describes as "cruel, wicked, foul, slanderous, and folly" in his public response to such accusations, published in *Household Words*, June 12, 1858:

> "Three and twenty years have passed since I entered on my present relations with the public. Through all that time I have tried to be as faithful to the public as they have been to me. It was my duty never to trifle with them, or deceive

them, or presume upon their favor, or do anything with it but to work hard to justify it.

My conspicuous position has often made me the subject of fabulous stories and unaccountable statements. Occasionally such things have chafed me, or even wounded me; but I have always accepted them as the shadows inseparable from the light of my notoriety and success. I have never obtruded any such personal uneasiness of mine, upon the generous aggregate of my audience.

CHARLES DICKENS
(PHOTO: ARCHIVIST, STOCK.ADOBE.COM)

For the first time in my life, and I believe for the last, I now deviate from this principle that I have so long observed, by presenting myself in my own journal, in my own private character, and entreating all my brethren (as they deem that they have reason to think well of me, and to know that I am a man who has ever been unaffectedly true to our common calling), to lend their aid to the dissemination of my present words.

Some domestic trouble of mine, of long-standing, on which I will make no further remark than that it claims to be respected, as being of a sacredly private nature, has lately been brought to an arrangement, which involves no anger or ill-will of any kind, and the whole origin, progress, and surrounding circumstances of which have been, throughout, within the knowledge of my children. It is amicably composed, and its details have now but to be forgotten by those concerning it.

By some means, arising out of wickedness, or out of folly, or out of inconceivable wild chance, or out of all three, this trouble has been made the occasion of misrepresentations, most grossly false, most monstrous, and most cruel—involving, not only me, but innocent persons dear to my heart, and innocent persons I have no knowledge, if, indeed, they have any existence—and so widely spread, that I doubt in one reader in a thousand will peruse these lines, by whom some touch of the breath of these slanderers will not have passed, like an unwholesome air.

Those who know me, and my nature, need no assurance under my hand that such calumnies are as irreconcilable with me, as they are, in their frantic incoherence, with one another. But, there is a great multitude who know me through my writings, and who do not know me otherwise; and I cannot bear that one of them should be left in doubt, or hazard of doubt, through my poorly shrinking from taking the unusual means to which I now resort, of circulating the truth.

I most solemnly declare, then—and this I do, both in my own name and my wife's name—that all the lately whispered rumors touching the trouble at which I have glanced, are abominably false. And that whosoever repeats one of them after this denial, will lie as willfully and as foully as it is possible for any false witness to lie, before Heaven and earth."

Though many spurious character sketches of Dickens have painted him in a less honorable light over the past 170 years, it should now be clear that these are misrepresentations of truth, and all who knew the Dickens's well had concurred, either in public or privately, in large degree with the narrative shared and published by Charles, and respected the fact that he went to such great lengths to protect, not only his own reputation, but those of his wife, his wife's sister, his servants, and his children.

DICKENS' CAREER TAKES OFF

A year later, in 1859, he released his epic classic. *A Tale of Two Cities*, still remains unrivaled in its honest depiction of the French Revolution—its causes and events, so truthfully and powerfully unfolded. The biblical truth our Lord teaches, "greater love hath no man than this, that he lay down his life for his friend" is a primary theme of the novel's eminent author.

Dickens was a gifted businessman as well as author, and managed to amass a large estate of wealth from the success of his writings, which he left in large measure to his children. He did experience difficulties with several American publishers who chose to underpay him and/or reprint some of his novels without permission or remuneration.

It was well known that he possessed strong political opinions, yet he was no mere partisan. Charles Dickens could have easily won a seat in the House of Commons, and any of the London boroughs would have been proud and glad to have him as its representative. Though numerous offers were made to him for such a position, he always declined—having resolved, early on in his career, to devote himself completely to literature. As the years rolled on, he recognized this approach being realized in that it brought him increase of power and influence upon the public mind more than ever, and if abuses were to be eliminated, wrongs righted, and reforms effected, it would be by his written words more than his spoken.

Since he was a young boy, Charles Dickens loved the stage and was quite versatile and gifted in his oratory and acting capabilities.

In latter years, it wasn't uncommon for him to entertain large groups on stage as well as smaller intimate groups of family and friends—especially well-received was his reading and acting of his Christmas stories during holiday occasions. His renown as an actor extended internationally, particularly being well received in America, having entertained large audiences in major U. S. cities such as Washington, Boston, New York, and Philadelphia.

Dickens read with touching expression and passion. However he may have begun, he had carefully and laboriously trained himself into reading to audiences in a natural and engaging style. His reading, in fact, was subdued acting—rarely demonstrative, but always what was called "telling." He threw himself into each character, shifting from one to the other with agile and surprising rapidity. He presented a unique grace that avoided professional elocution, but he instead read as a highly cultivated gentleman might be expected to read, in a private drawing room, to ladies and gentlemen of equally high culture. Above all, he was not stagey. His one peculiarity was that it was his pattern to close each sentence with a rising inflection, quick and sharp. This is the English habit of intonation, which he had as part of his style. The readings had been quite successful, in reputation as well as in worldly gain. His manner of reading was extraordinary in that he would typically present from memory. Though he had the printed text always ready for instant reference, in the event of his memory failed to supply the required word, but it is believed that constant repetition had engraved each sentence upon his mind.

HIS FINAL WORKS AND DEPARTURE

In the early months of 1870, Dickens experienced increasing bouts of pain in his feet, which would prohibit him from attending to his performance schedule. In May, just a short time before complications from this illness would take his life, he had made significant progress on his final work of fiction, *The Mystery of Edwin Drood*, and knowing declining health was upon him, was anxious to complete the novel.

Dickens often expressed a longing for a sudden death, and he was not a man to assert an opinion for mere word's sake. Sheldon MacKenzie shared: "A friend told us that while walking across Kensington Gardens one day with Dickens, a thunder storm suddenly came. As the rain began to descend, the great novelist proposed shelter beneath the trees. 'No,' said his heroic but timid friend, 'that is too dangerous.' Many people have been killed beneath trees from the effects of lightning.' 'Well,' said Dickens, turning and looking earnestly at his friend, 'of all the fears that harass a man on God's earth, the fear of sudden death seems to me the most absurd. Why we pray against it in the Litany I cannot make out. A death by lightning most resembles the translation of Enoch [Gen. 5:21-24]."

In God's providence, these words of Charles Dickens became somewhat of a reality in his own "home going." The illness that took him from us was an illness unto death and did its work quickly. He died quietly in his home on June 9, 1870, having made a lasting impact on the hearts and minds of his hearers and readers for over three decades. He was a man of supreme talent for story telling, but his passion went well beyond the message. It was to bring true-to-life events and actions before his audiences, exposing the realities of man's heart both good and evil—and that the primary reforming agent is faith in God—thus making the world a better place.

DICKENS' STUDY AT GADS HILL HOUSE

When the news of his death reached Queen Victoria, she sent a telegram to Gad's Hill House, expressing her deepest sorrow. Other members of the royal family and other nobility of all ranks and classes did the same. A national loss had been sustained and in that hour of sorrow the country spoke as with one voice. The dead man had been, in his works, a welcome guest in every household. It was not his intention to set class against class, yet he had always been the champion of the poor, the oppressed and the afflicted. It was one consolation for his family that, though his purse was ever open for benevolent purposes, he left ample provision for his family. It had been his often expressed wish that his mortal remains should be deposited at Rochester, in the shadow of the fine old Cathedral the Cloisterham of his last, and unfinished story. Preparations were made for seeing this accomplished, except *The Times*, on June llth, suggested that Westminster Abbey, the British Pantheon of England, was the proper place for the sepulture for England's great author. By a coincidence of thought, which is not inexplicable, the same suggestion was made in the Washington Chronicle the very same day. Mr. Gladstone eagerly sustained the suggestion, the Dean of Westminster also approving of it.

Mr. Dickens had directed, in his will, that his funeral should be "unostentatious, and strictly private," and that his friends should not make him "the subject of any monument, memorial, or testimonial whatever." His family, weighing these words, came to the conclusion that neither their letter nor spirit would be violated by a private interment in Poets' Corner, Westminster Abbey.

The eminent Reverend Arthur Penrhyn Stanley, DD, delivered the funeral sermon honoring the memory and influence of Charles Dickens on June 18, 1870.

THE LIFE OF OUR LORD

DICKENS' LAST PUBLIC READING

DICKENS' INFLUENCE THROUGH HIS FAITH, LIFE, AND WRITINGS

It is quite fitting that the Scripture text selected for the sermon at the funeral of Charles Dickens was the parable of Lazarus and the Rich man—for it, more than any other of Christ's parables, presents the sharp contrast between those who live in this world serving themselves at the expense of others less fortunate and therefore receive the eternal judgment of Hell, and the poor of this world whose suffering is replaced in the next, with everlasting bliss, through faith in Christ. The following is several poignant excerpts in regards to the rich impact Dickens' faith and writings had on the world:

> "In no age of the world, and in no country of the world, has been developed on so large a scale, and with such striking

effects as in our own, the gift of 'speaking in parables;' the gift of addressing mankind through romance and novel and tale and fable."

"In his long series of stirring tales, now for ever closed, there was a profoundly serious, nay, may we not say, a profoundly Christian and evangelical truth of which we all need to be reminded, and of which he was, in his own way, the special teacher."

"It was a fine trait of a noble character of our own times, that, though full of interests, intellectual, domestic, social, the distress of the poor of England, he used to say, 'pierced through his happiness and haunted him day and night.' It is because this susceptibility is so rare, so difficult to attain, that we ought doubly to value those who have the eye to see, and the ear to hear, and the tongue to speak, and the pen to describe, those who are not at hand to demand their own rights, to set forth their own wrongs, to portray their own sufferings. Such was he who lies yonder. By him that veil was rent asunder which parts the various classes of society. Through his genius the rich man, faring sumptuously every day, was made to see and feel the presence of the Lazarus at his gate. The unhappy inmates of the workhouse, the neglected children in the dens and caves of our great cities, the starved and ill-used boys in remote schools, far from the observation of men, felt that a new ray of sunshine was poured on their dark existence, a new interest awakened in their forlorn and desolate lot. It was because an unknown friend had pleaded their cause with a voice, which rang through the palaces of the great, as well as through the cottages of the poor. It was because, as by a magician's wand, those gaunt figures and strange faces had been, it may be sometimes, in exaggerated forms, made to stand and speak before those who hardly dreamed of their existence."

"He labored to tell us all, in new, very new words, the old, old story that there is even in the worst of capacity for goodness a soul worth redeeming, worth reclaiming, worth regenerating. He labored to tell the rich, the educated, how this better side was to be found and respected even in the most neglected Lazarus. He labored to tell the poor no less, to respect this better part in themselves, to remember that they also have a call to be good and just, if they will but hear it. If by any such means he has brought rich and poor nearer together, and made Englishmen feel more nearly as one family, he will not assuredly have lived in vain, nor will his bones in vain have been laid in this home and hearth of the English nation."

"After the emphatic injunctions respecting 'the inexpensive, unostentatious, and strictly private 'manner' of his funeral", which were carried out to the very letter, he thus instructed: "I direct that my name be inscribed in plain English letters on my tomb . . . I conjure my friends on no account to make me the subject of any monument, memorial, or testimonial whatever. I rest my claims to the remembrance of my country upon my published works, and to the remembrance of my friends upon their experience of me in addition thereto. I commit my soul to the mercy of God through our Lord and Saviour Jesus Christ; and I exhort my dear children humbly to try to guide themselves by the teaching of the New Testament in its broad spirit, and to put no faith in any man's narrow construction of its letter here or there."

"In that simple but sufficient faith he lived and died; in that faith he bids you live and die. If any of you have learned from his works the value, the eternal value of generosity, purity, kindness, unselfishness, and have learned to show these in your own hearts and lives, these are the best monuments, memorials, and testimonials of the friend whom you loved, and who loved, with a rare and touching love, his friends, his country, and his fellowmen: monuments which he would not refuse, and which the humblest, the poorest, the youngest have it in their power to raise to his memory."

In the mercy of God, Dickens lived to see the abolishment of imprisonment for debt in his own country, and the hear others say on his behalf, "You have done this!"

Mackenzie continues in his biography: "Believing that the world has been made brighter and better by the writings and life of Charles Dickens, I can have no hesitation in briefly delineating his character, as author and as a man. In the whole range, vast as it is, which constitutes the common literature, the rich treasury, of America and England, not to speak of the numerous languages into which they have been translated, there are no purer books than those written by Charles Dickens. There is no line in them which the most scrupulous parent, the most tender husband, the most sensitive lover, the most fastidious guardian could desire to keep back from the eye of Maidenhood or Womanhood. There are no other works, in the language, so well adapted for all classes and all ages. They may be taken up, at any place or time, and the reader will be gratified by the entertainment they supply, the moral lesson, which they teach: Age cannot wither them, nor custom stale their infinite variety. No writer has more completely, or more successfully, appealed to the emotional and sympathetic part of human nature. It is doubtful, as he glanced from glee to grave, whether his lively humor or his tender pathos was most to be admired. Whatever vein he indulged in, for the time, he avoided cynicism. Hence, we laugh with, instead of at, his comic characters, taking Pickwick, and Sam Weller, and Wilkins Micawber, and Mr. Toots, and Dick Swiveller, and Captain Cuttle, (that truest of all rough gentlemen,) to our heart, and feeling all the better for having met, and known, and loved them."

The heart of Dickens as expressed in his fiction can be well summed up in his own words: "Only God knows how a man can impose upon himself. Human experience bears this out unmistakably; and yet human beings with all their experience, continue blind to their own frailties, and while they are forever taking the mote out of the eye of another, willfully refuse to see the beam, which is in their own. The beam is often plainly manifest, but politeness, interest, dependency, and many other reasons incline their associates to tolerate it rather than incur their displeasure by pointing it out. The Word of God threshes out these things unequivocally, but unhappily, men do not recognize themselves in the portraits delineated therein, notwithstanding their scrupulous fidelity. They see apostate Jews, and godless gentiles, and faithless disciples of a past age; they hear warnings and judgments threatened against such generations, and marvel at the hypocrisies of the Scribes and Pharisees, but overlook the tremendous fact that under their robes and phylacteries breathed the same nature, which exists beneath the coat and trousers of the nineteenth century. To drive home this truth in modern garments and with modern surroundings, to show men themselves actuated by the mean hypocritical motives which they either have resolutely blinded themselves to the existence of, or else fondly imagine they are successfully concealing from the world, is to go over the same ground that the Bible has covered."

With this belief and spirit did Charles Dickens thus write. Furthermore, the wickedness and oppression of evildoers painted by Dickens are constantly unmasked and eventually punished, often by small degrees to add emphasis on its import and poignantly set the stage for it resolution within his narrative. Only then the cause of the weak, abused, poor, and needy can be so powerfully championed. This was the genius of Charles Dickens and catalyst for cultivating the formation of good character and virtue within society.

THE MAJOR WORKS OF CHARLES DICKENS

- *Sketches of Boz* (1833-1836)
- *Pickwick Papers* (1836-1837)
- *Oliver Twist* (1837-1839)
- *Nicholas Nickleby* (1838-1839)
- *The Old Curiosity Shop* (1840-1841)
- *Barnaby Rudge* (1841)
- *Martin Chuzzlewit* (1843-1844)
- *A Christmas Carol* (1843)
- *Dombey and Son* (1846-1848)
- *The Life of Our Lord* (1849)
- *David Copperfield* (1848-1850)
- *Bleak House* (1851-1853)
- *Hard Times* (1854)
- *Little Dorrit* (1855-1857)
- *A Tale of Two Cities* (1859)
- *Great Expectations* (1860-1861)
- *Our Mutual Friend* (1864-1865)
- *Edwin Drood* (1870)

BIOGRAPHICAL REFERENCES

- *Life of Charles Dickens,* by R. Shelton MacKenzie (1870)
- *The Life of Charles Dickens,* by John Forster (1871)
- *The Religious Sentiments of Charles Dickens,* by Charles McKenzie (1884)

The Life of Our Lord
by Charles Dickens

A FACSIMILE OF THE FIRST PAGE OF THE MANUSCRIPT OF CHARLES DICKENS' LIFE OF OUR LORD

THE NATIVITY

*"And they came with haste, and found Mary and Joseph,
and the babe lying in a manger."*
—Luke 2:16

Chapter the First

MY DEAR CHILDREN,

I am very anxious that you should know something about the history of Jesus Christ. For everybody ought to know about Him. No one ever lived, who was so good, so kind, so gentle, and so sorry for all people who did wrong, or were in any way ill or miserable, as He was. He is now in Heaven, where we hope to go, and all to meet each other after we are dead, and there be happy always together. You never can imagine what a good place Heaven is without knowing who He was and what He did.

He was born a long, long time ago—nearly two thousand years ago—at a place called Bethlehem. His father and mother lived in a city called Nazareth, but they were forced, by business, to travel to Bethlehem. His father's name was Joseph, and his mother's name was Mary. And the town being very full of people, also brought there by business, there was no room for Joseph and Mary in the Inn or in any house; so they went into a stable to lodge, and in this stable Jesus Christ was born. There was no cradle or anything of that kind there, so Mary layed her pretty little boy in what is called the Manger, which is the place the horses eat out of. And there He fell asleep.

While He was asleep, some Shepherds who were watching sheep in the fields, saw an angel from God, all light and beautiful, come moving over the grass towards them. At first they were afraid and fell down and hid their faces. But it said "There is a child born today in the City of Bethlehem near here, who will grow up to be so good that God will love him as his own Son; and He will teach men to love one another, and not to quarrel and hurt one another; and his name will be Jesus Christ; and people will put that name in their prayers, because they will know God loves Him, and will know that they should love Him too." And then the angel told the shepherds to go to that stable, and look at the little child in the manger, which they did; and they kneeled down by it in its sleep, and said, "God bless this child!"

Now the great place of all that country was Jerusalem—just as London is the great place in England—and at Jerusalem the King lived, whose name was King Herod. Some wise men came one day, from a country a long way off in the East, and said to the King, "We have seen a Star in the sky, which shows us that a child is born in Bethlehem who will live to be a man whom all people will love." When King Herod heard this, he was jealous, for he was a wicked man. But he pretended not to be jealous, and said to the wise men, "Whereabouts is this child?" And the wise men said, "We don't know, but we think the star will show us; for the star has been moving on before us, all the way here, and is now standing still in the sky." Then Herod asked them to see if the Star would show them where the child lived, and ordered them, if

CHAPTER THE FIRST

they found the child, to come back to him. So they went out, and the Star went on, over their heads a little way before them, until it stopped over the house where the child was. This was very wonderful, but God ordered it to be so.

When the Star stopped, the wise men went in, and saw the child with Mary, his Mother. They loved him very much, and gave him some presents. Then they went away. But they did not go back to King Herod; for they thought he was jealous, though he had not said so. So they went away, by night, back into their own country. And an Angel came, and told Joseph and Mary to take the child into a country called Egypt, or Herod would kill him. So they escaped too, in the night—the father, the mother, and the child—and arrived there, safely. But when this cruel Herod found that the wise men did not come back to him, and that he could not, therefore, find out where this child, Jesus Christ, lived, he called his soldiers and captains to him, and told them to go and kill all the children in his dominions that were not more than two years old. The wicked men did so. The mothers of the children ran up and down the streets with them in their arms trying to save them, and hide them in caves and cellars, but it was of no use. The soldiers with their swords killed all the children they could find. This dreadful murder was called the Murder of the Innocents, because the little children were so innocent. King Herod hoped that Jesus Christ was one of them. But He was not, as you know, for He had escaped safely into Egypt. And he lived there, with his father and mother, until bad King Herod died.

JESUS WITH THE DOCTORS

"And He said unto them, How is it that you sought me? Do you not know that I must be about my father's business?"
—Luke 2:49

Chapter the Second

WHEN KING HEROD was dead, an angel came to Joseph again, and said he might now go to Jerusalem, and not be afraid for the child's sake. So Joseph and Mary, and her Son Jesus Christ (who are commonly called the Holy Family) travelled towards Jerusalem. But hearing on the way that King Herod's son was the new King, and fearing that he too might want to hurt the child, they turned out of the way, and went to live in Nazareth. They lived there until Jesus Christ was twelve years old. Then Joseph and Mary went to Jerusalem to attend a religious feast, which used to be held in those days in the Temple of Jerusalem, which was a great church or cathedral; and they took Jesus Christ with them. And when the feast was over, they travelled away from Jerusalem, back towards their own home in Nazareth, with a great many of their friends and neighbors. For people used to travel a great many together, for fear of robbers; the roads not being so safe and well guarded as they are now, and travelling being much more difficult altogether, than it is now.

They travelled on for a whole day and never knew that Jesus Christ was not with them; for the company being so large, they thought He was somewhere among the people, though they did not see Him. But finding that He was not there, and fearing that He was lost, they turned back to Jerusalem in great anxiety to look for Him. They found Him, sitting in the temple, talking about the goodness of God, and how we should all pray to Him, along with some learned men who were called doctors. They were not what you understand by the word "doctors" now, they did not attend sick people, and they were scholars and clever men. And Jesus Christ showed such knowledge in what He said to them, and in the questions He asked them, that they were all astonished.

He went home to Nazareth, with Joseph and Mary, when they had found Him, and lived there until He was thirty or thirty-five years old.

At that time there was a very good man indeed, named John, who was the son of a woman named Elizabeth, the cousin of Mary. And people being wicked and violent, and killing each other, and not minding their duty towards God, John (to teach them better) went about the country, preaching to them, and entreating them to be better men and women. And because he loved them more than himself, and didn't mind himself when he was doing them good, he was poorly dressed in the skin of a camel, and ate little but some insects called locusts, which he found as he travelled, and wild honey, which the bees left in the hollow trees. You never saw a locust, because they belong to that country near Jerusalem, which is a great way off. So do camels, but I think you have seen a camel at all events, they are brought over here, sometimes; and if you would like to see one, I will show you one.

CHAPTER THE SECOND

There was a river, not very far from Jerusalem, called the River Jordan; and in this water John baptized those people who would come to him, and promise to be better. A great many people went to him in crowds. Jesus Christ went too. But when John saw him, John said, "Why should I baptize you, who are so much better than I!" Jesus Christ made answer, "Suffer it to be so now." So John baptized Him. And when He was baptized, the sky opened, and a beautiful bird like a dove came flying down, and the voice of God, speaking up in Heaven, was heard to say, "This is my beloved Son, in whom I am well pleased!"

Then Jesus Christ went into a wild and lonely country called the wilderness, and stayed there forty days and forty nights, praying that He might be of use to men and women, and teach them to be better, so that after their deaths, they might be happy in Heaven.

When He came out of the wilderness, He began to cure sick people by only laying His hand upon them; for God had given Him power to heal the sick, and to give sight to the blind, and to do many wonderful and solemn things of which I shall tell you more bye and bye, and which are called the Miracles of Christ. I wish you would remember that word, because I shall use it again, and I should like you to know that it means something very wonderful and which could not be done without God's leave and assistance.

The first miracle that Jesus Christ did was at a place called Cana, where He went to a marriage-feast with Mary His mother. There was no wine and Mary told Him so. There were only six stone water-pots filled with water. But Jesus turned this water into wine by only lifting up His hand; and all who were there drank of it.

For God had given Jesus Christ the power to do such wonders; and He did them, that people might know He was not a common man, and might believe what He taught them, and also believe that God had sent Him. And many people, hearing this, and hearing that He cured the sick, did begin to believe in Him; and great crowds followed Him in the streets and on the roads, wherever He went.

JESUS HEALING THE SICK

"And great multitudes came unto Him, having with them those that were lame, blind, dumb, maimed, and many others, and cast them down at Jesus feet; and He healed them."
—Matthew 15:30

Chapter the Third

THAT THERE MIGHT be some good men to go about with Him, teaching the people, Jesus Christ chose twelve poor men to be His companions. These twelve are called the Apostles or Disciples, and He chose them from among poor men, in order that the poor might know—always after that, in all years to come—that Heaven was made for them as well as for the rich, and that God makes no difference between those who wear good clothes and those who go barefoot and in rags. The most miserable, the most ugly, deformed, wretched creatures that live, will be bright Angels in Heaven if they are good here on earth. Never forget this, when you are grown up. Never be proud or unkind, my dears, to any poor man, woman, or child. If they are bad, think that they would have been better if they had kind friends, and good homes, and had been better taught. So, always try to make them better by kind, persuading words; and always try to teach them and relieve them if you can. And when people speak ill of the poor and miserable, think how Jesus Christ went among them, and taught them, and thought them worthy of His care. And always pity them yourselves, and think as well of them as you can.

The names of the twelve Apostles were Simon Peter, Andrew, James the son of Zebedee, John, Philip, Bartholomew, Thomas, Matthew, James the son of Alphaeus, Labbaeus, Simon, and Judas Iscariot. This man afterwards betrayed Jesus Christ, as you will hear bye and bye.

The first four of these were poor fishermen, who were sitting in their boats by the seaside, mending their nets, when Christ passed by. He stopped and went into Simon Peter's boat, and asked him if he had caught many fish. Peter said No; though they had worked all night with their nets, they had caught nothing. Christ said, "Let down the net again." They did so; and it was immediately so full of fish, that it required the strength of many men (who came and helped them) to lift it out of the water, and even then it was very hard to do. This was another of the Miracles of Jesus Christ.

Jesus then said, "Come with me," and they followed Him directly. And from that time the twelve Disciples or Apostles were always with Him.

As great crowds of people followed Him, and wished to be taught, He went up into a mountain, and there preached to them, and gave them, from His own lips, the words of that prayer, beginning, "Our Father which art in Heaven," that you say every night. It is called the Lord's Prayer because it was first spoken by Jesus Christ, and because He commanded His Disciples to pray in those words.

When He was come down from the mountain, there came to Him a man with a dreadful disease called leprosy. It was common in those times; and those who were ill with it were called lepers. This leper fell at the feet of Jesus Christ, and said, "Lord! If You will, You can make me well!" Jesus, always full of compassion, stretched out His hand, and said, "I will! Be well!" And his disease went away, immediately, and he was cured.

Being followed wherever He went, by great crowds of people, Jesus went with His Disciples into a house to rest. While He was sitting inside, some men brought upon a bed a man who was very ill of what he called the palsy, so that he trembled all over from head to foot, and could neither stand nor move. But the crowd being all about the doors and windows, and they not being able to get near Jesus Christ, these men climbed up to the roof of the house, which was a low one; and through the tiling at the top, let down the bed, with the sick man upon it, into the room where Jesus sat. When He saw him, Jesus, full of pity, said, "Arise! Take up your bed, and go to your own home!" And the man rose up and went away quite well, blessing Him, and thanking God.

There was a centurion too, or officer over the soldiers, who came to him and said, "Lord! My servant lies at home in my house, very ill." Jesus Christ answered, "I will come and cure him." But the centurion said, "Lord! I am not worthy that You should come to my house. Say the word only, and I know he will be cured." Then Jesus Christ, glad that the centurion believed in Him so truly, said, "Be it so!" And the servant became well, from that moment.

But of all the people who came to Him, none was so full of grief and distress, as one man who was a ruler or magistrate over many people, and he wrung his hands, and cried, and said, "O Lord, my daughter, my beautiful, good, innocent little girl, is dead. Oh come to her, come to her, and lay your blessed hand upon her, and I know she will revive, and come to life again, and make her mother and me happy. O Lord, we love her so, we love her so! And she is dead!"

Jesus Christ went out with him, and so did His Disciples, and went to his house, where the friends and neighbors were crying in the room where the poor dead little girl lay, and where there was soft music playing; as there used to be, in those days, when people died. Jesus Christ, looking on her sorrowfully, said to comfort her poor parents "She is not dead. She is asleep," Then He commanded the room to be cleared of the people that were in it, and going to the dead child, took her by the hand, and she rose up, quite well, as if she had only been asleep. Oh, what a sight it must have been to see her parents clasp her in their arms, and kiss her, and thank God and Jesus Christ, His Son, for such great mercy!

But He was always merciful and tender. And because He did such good, and taught people how to love God and how to hope to go to Heaven after death, he was called Our Saviour.

JESUS STILLING THE TEMPEST

"And He arose, and rebuked the wind, and said unto the sea, 'Peace by still!' And the wind ceased, and there was a great calm."
—Mark 4:39

Chapter the Fourth

THERE WERE IN that country, where our saviour performed His miracles, certain people who were called Pharisees. They were very proud, and believed that no people were good but themselves; and they were all afraid of Jesus Christ, because He taught the people better. So were the Jews, in general. Most of the inhabitants of that country were Jews.

Our Saviour, walking once in the fields with His Disciples on a Sunday (which the Jews called, and still call, the Sabbath) they gathered some ears of the corn that was growing there, to eat. This, the Pharisees said, was wrong; and in the same way, when Our Saviour went into one of their churches, they were called synagogues, and looked compassionately on a poor man who had his hand all withered and wasted away, these Pharisees said, "Is it right to cure people on a Sunday?" Our Saviour answered them by saying, "If any of you had a sheep, and it fell into a pit, would you not take it out, even though it happened on a Sunday? And how much better is a man than a sheep!" Then He said to the poor man, "Stretch out your hand!" And it was cured immediately, and was smooth and useful like the other. So Jesus Christ told them, "You may always do good, no matter what the day is."

There was a city called Nain into which Our Saviour went soon after this, followed by great numbers of people, and especially by those who had sick relations, or friends, or children. For they brought sick people out into the streets and roads through which He passed, and cried out to Him to touch them; and when He did, they became well. Going on, in the midst of this crowd, and near the gate of the city, He met a funeral. It was the funeral of a young man, who was carried on what is called a bier, which was open, as the custom was in that country, and is now in many parts of Italy. His poor mother followed the bier, and wept very much, for she had no other child. When Our Saviour saw her, He was touched to the heart to see her so sorry, and said, "Weep not!" Then, as the bearers of the bier stood still, He walked up to it and touched it with His hand, and said, "Young man! Arise!" The dead man, coming to life again at the sound of the Saviour's voice, rose up and began to speak. And Jesus Christ, leaving him with his mother—ah how happy they both were!—went away.

By this time the crowd was so very great that Jesus Christ went down to the waterside, to go in a boat, to a more retired place. And in the boat He fell asleep, while His Disciples were sitting on the deck. While He was still sleeping, a violent storm arose, so that the waves washed over the boat, and the howling wind so rocked and shook it, that they thought it would sink. In their fright the Disciples awoke Our Saviour, and said, "Lord! Save us, or we are lost!" He stood up, and raising His arm, said to the rolling sea and to the whistling wind, "Peace! Be still!" And

CHAPTER THE FOURTH

immediately it was calm and pleasant weather, and the boat went safely on through the smooth waters.

When they came to the other side of the waters they had to pass a wild and lonely burying-ground that was outside the city to which they were going. All burying-grounds were outside cities in those times. In this place there was a dreadful madman who lived among the tombs, and howled all day and night, that it made travellers afraid to hear him. They had tried to chain him, but he broke his chains, he was so strong. He would throw himself on the sharp stones, and cut himself in the most dreadful manner, crying and howling all the while. When this wretched man saw Jesus Christ a long way off, he cried out, "It is the Son of God! Oh, Son of God, do not torment me!" Jesus, coming near him, perceived that he was torn by an evil spirit, and cast the madness out of him, and into a herd of swine (or pigs) who were feeding close by, and who directly ran headlong down a steep place leading into the sea, and were dashed to pieces.

Now Herod, the son of that cruel King who murdered the Innocents, reigning over the people there, and hearing that Jesus Christ was doing these wonders, and was giving sight to the blind, and causing the deaf to hear, and the dumb to speak, and the lame to walk, and that He was followed by multitudes and multitudes of people Herod, hearing this, said: "This man is a companion and friend of John the Baptist." John was the good man, you recollect, who wore a garment made of camel's hair, and ate wild honey. Herod had taken him prisoner, because he taught and preached to the people; and had him then locked up, in the prisons of his palace.

While Herod was in this angry humour with John, his

birthday came; and his daughter Herodias, who was a fine dancer, danced before him, to please him. She pleased him so much that he swore an oath that he would give her whatever she would ask him for. "Then," she said, "father, give me the head of John the Baptist in a charger," for she hated John, and was a wicked, cruel woman.

The King was sorry, for though he had John prisoner, he did not wish to kill him, but having sworn that he would give her what she asked for, he sent some soldiers down into the prison, with directions to cut off the head of John the Baptist, and give it to Herodias. This they did, and took it to her, as she had said, in a charger, which was a kind of dish. When Jesus Christ heard from the Apostles of this cruel deed, He left that city, and went with them (after they had privately buried John's body in the night) to another place.

SERMON ON THE MOUNT

*"You are the light of the world.
A city that is set on a hill cannot be hidden."*
—Matthew 5:14

Chapter the Fifth

ONE OF THE pharisees begged our saviour to go into his house, and eat with him.

And while Our Saviour sat eating at the table, there crept into the room a woman of that city who had led a bad and sinful life, and was ashamed that the Son of God should see her; and yet she trusted so much to His goodness and His compassion for all who, having done wrong were truly sorry for it in their hearts, that, by little and little, she went behind the seat on which He had sat, and dropped down at His feet, and wetted them with her sorrowful tears; then she kissed them, and dried them on her long hair, and rubbed them with some sweet-smelling ointment she had brought with her in a box. Her name was Mary Magdalene.

When the Pharisee saw that Jesus permitted this woman to touch Him, he said within himself that Jesus did not know how wicked she had been. But Jesus Christ, who knew His thoughts, said to him, "Simon, if a man had debtors, one of whom owed him five hundred pence, and one of whom owed him only fifty pence, and he forgave them, both their debts, which of those two debtors do you think would love him most?"

Simon answered, "I suppose that one whom he forgave most." Jesus told him he was right, and said, "As God forgives this woman so much sin, she will love Him, I hope, the more." And He said to her, "God forgives you!" The company who were present wondered that Jesus Christ had power to forgive sins, but God had given it to Him. And the woman, thanking Him for all His mercy, went away.

We learn from this that we must always forgive those who have done us any harm, when they come to us and say they are truly sorry for it. Even if they do not come and say so, we must still forgive them, and never hate them or be unkind to them, if we would hope for God to forgive us.

After this, there was a great feast of the Jews, and Jesus Christ went to Jerusalem.

Near the sheep market in that place, there was a pool, or pond, called Bethesda, having five gates to it. At the time of the year when that feast took place great numbers of sick people and cripples went to this pool to bathe in it: believing that an Angel came and stirred the water, and that whoever went in first after the Angel had done so, was cured of any illness he or she had, whatever it might be. Among those poor persons was one man who had been ill for thirty-eight years; and he told Jesus Christ (who took pity on him when He saw him lying on his bed alone, with no one to help him) that he never could be dipped in the pool, because he was so weak and ill that he could not move to get there.

Our Saviour said to him, "Take up your bed and go away,"

and he went away, quite well. Many Jews saw this; and when they saw it, they hated Jesus Christ the more: knowing that the people, being taught and cured by Him, would not believe their priests, who told the people what was not true, and deceived them. So they said to one another that Jesus Christ should be killed, because He cured people on the Sabbath Day (which was against their strict law) and because He called Himself the Son of God. And they tried to raise enemies against Him, and to stir the crowd in the streets to murder Him.

But the crowd followed Him wherever He went, blessing Him, and praying to be taught and cured; for they knew He did nothing but good. Jesus, going with His Disciples over a sea, called the Sea of Tiberias, and sitting with them on a hill-side, saw great numbers of these poor people waiting below, and said to the Apostle Philip, "Where shall we buy bread, that they may eat and be refreshed, after their long journey?" Philip answered, "Lord, two hundred pennyworth of bread would not be enough for so many people, and we have none." "We have only five small barley loaves, and two little fish, belonging to a lad who is among us," said another Apostle Andrew. "What are they, among so many!" Jesus Christ said, "Let them all sit down!" They did, there being a great deal of grass in that place. When they were all seated, Jesus took the bread, and looked up to Heaven, and blessed it, and broke it, and handed it in pieces to the Apostles, who handed it to the people. And of those five little loaves and two fish, five thousand men, besides women, and children, ate, and had enough; and when they were all satisfied, there were gathered up twelve baskets full of what was left. This was another of the miracles of Jesus Christ.

Our Saviour then sent His Disciples away in a boat, across the water, and said He would follow them presently, when He had dismissed the people. The people being gone, He remained by himself to pray. The night came on, and the Disciples were still rowing on the water in their boat, wondering when Christ would come. Late in the night, when the wind rose up against them and the waves were running high, they saw Him coming, walking towards them on the water, as if it were dry land. When they saw this, they were terrified, and cried out, but Jesus said, "It is I, be not afraid!" Peter taking courage, said, "Lord, if it is You, tell me to come to You upon the water." Jesus Christ said, "Come!" Peter then walked towards Him, but seeing the angry waves, and hearing the wind roar, he was frightened and began to sink, and would have done so, but Jesus took him by the hand and led him into the boat. Then, in a moment, the wind went down; and the Disciples said to one another, "It is true! He is the Son of God!"

Jesus did many more miracles after this happened and cured the sick in great numbers, making the lame walk, and the dumb speak, and the blind see. And being again surrounded by a great crowd who were faint and hungry, and had been with Him for three days, eating little, He took from His Disciples seven loaves and a few fish, and again divided them among the people, who were four thousand in number. They all ate, and had enough; and of what was left there were gathered up seven baskets full.

He now divided the Disciples, and sent them into many towns and villages, teaching the people, and giving them power to cure, in the name of God, all those who were ill. And at this time He began to tell them (for He knew what would happen) that He must one day go back to Jerusalem where He would suffer a great deal, and where He would certainly be put to death. But He said to them that on the third day after He was dead, He would rise from the grave, and ascend to Heaven, where He would sit at the right hand of God, beseeching God's pardon to sinners.

THE WOMAN RECEIVES FORGIVENESS

"He raised himself up and said the them, 'He who is without sin among you, let him first cast a stone at her.'"
—John 8:7

Chapter the Sixth

SIX DAYS AFTER the last miracle of the loaves and fish, Jesus Christ went up into a high mountain, with only three of the Disciples Peter, James, and John. And while He was speaking to them there, suddenly His face began to shine as if it were the sun, and the robes He wore, which were white, glistened and shone like sparkling silver, and He stood before them like an Angel. A bright cloud overshadowed them at the same time; and a voice, speaking from the cloud, was heard to say, "This is My beloved Son in whom I am well pleased. Hear Him!" At which the three Disciples fell on their knees and covered their faces, being afraid. This is called the Transfiguration of Our Saviour.

When they came down from this mountain, and were among the people again, a man knelt at the feet of Jesus Christ, and said, "Lord, have mercy on my son, for he is mad and cannot help himself, and sometimes falls into the fire, and sometimes into the water, and covers himself with scars and sores. Some of your

Disciples have tried to cure him, but could not." Our Saviour cured the child immediately; and, turning to His Disciples, told them they had not been able to cure him themselves, because they did not believe in Him so truly as He had hoped.

The Disciples asked Him, "Master, who is greatest in the Kingdom of Heaven?" Jesus called a little child to Him, and took him in His arms, and stood among them, and answered, "A child like this. I say unto you that none but those who are as humble as little children shall enter into Heaven. Whosoever shall receive one such little child in my name receives me. But whosoever hurts one of them, it would be better for him if he had a millstone tied about his neck, and be drowned in the depths of the sea." The Angels are all like children. Our Saviour loved the child and loves all children. Yes, and loves the world. No one ever loved people, so well and so truly as He did.

Peter asked Him, "Lord, how often shall I forgive any one who offends me? Seven times?" Our Saviour answered, "Seventy times seven times, and more than that. For how can you hope that God will forgive you, when you do wrong, unless you forgive all other people!"

And He told His Disciples this story: He said, "There was once a servant who owed his master a great deal of money, and could not pay it, at which the master, being very angry, was going to have this servant sold for a slave. But the servant kneeling down and begging his master's pardon with great sorrow, the master forgave him. Now this same servant had a fellow servant who owed him a hundred pence, and instead of being kind and forgiving to this poor man, as his master had been to him, he put him in prison for the debt. His master, hearing of it, went

CHAPTER THE SIXTH

to him, and said, 'O wicked servant, I forgave you. Why did you not forgive your fellow-servant?' And because he had not done so, his master turned him away, with great misery. So," said Our Saviour, "how can you expect God to forgive you, if you do not forgive others?" This is the meaning of that part of the Lord's Prayer, where we say "Forgive us our trespasses" that word means faults "as we forgive them that trespass against us."

And He told them another story, and said; "There was a certain farmer once, who had a vineyard, and he went out early in the morning, and agreed with some labourers to work there, all day, for a penny. And bye and bye, when it was later, he went out again and engaged some more labourers on the same terms; and bye and bye went out again; and so on, several times, until the afternoon. When the day was over, and they all came to be paid, those who had worked since morning complained that those who had not begun to work until late in the day had the same money as themselves, and they said it was not fair. But the master said, 'Friend, I agreed with you for a penny; and is it less money to you, because I give the same money to another man?'"

Our Saviour meant to teach them by this, that people who have done well all their lives long would go to Heaven after they are dead. But that people who have been wicked, because of their being miserable, or not having parents and friends to take care of them when young, and who are truly sorry for it, however late in their lives, and pray God to forgive them, will be forgiven and will go to Heaven too. He taught His Disciples in these stories, because He knew the people liked to hear them, and would remember what He said better, if He said it in that way. They are called Parables—The Parables of our Saviour; and I wish you to remember that word, as I shall soon have some more of these parables to tell you about.

The people listened to all that Our Saviour said, but they did not agree among themselves about Him. The Pharisees and Jews had spoken to some of them against Him, and some of them were inclined to do Him harm and even to murder Him. But they were afraid, as yet, to do Him any harm, because of His goodness, and His looking so divine and grand although he was very simply dressed, almost like the poor people that they could hardly bear to meet His eyes.

One morning He was sitting in a place called the Mount of Olives, teaching the people who were all clustered round Him, listening and learning attentively, when a great noise was heard, and a crowd of Pharisees, and some other people like them, called Scribes, came running in, with great cries and shouts, dragging among them a woman who had done wrong. They all cried out together, "Master! Look at this woman. The law says she shall be pelted with stones until she is dead. But what say you? What say you?"

Jesus looked upon the noisy crowd attentively, and knew that they had come to make Him say the law was wrong and cruel; and that if He said so, they would make it a charge against Him and would kill Him. They were ashamed and afraid as He looked into their faces, but they still cried out, "Come! What say you, Master? What say you?"

Jesus stooped down, and wrote with His finger in the sand on the ground. He then raised himself up and said to them, "He that is without sin among you, let him throw the first stone at her." Jesus stooped down again and wrote in the sand, and they went

CHAPTER THE SIXTH

away, one by one, ashamed, until not a man of all the noisy crowd was left there; and Jesus Christ and the woman, hiding her face in her hands, alone remained.

Then Jesus said, "Woman, where are your accusers? Has no man condemned you?" She answered, trembling. "No, Lord!" "Then," said Our Saviour, "neither do I condemn you. Go! And Sin no more!"

LAZARUS AND THE RICH MAN

"And there was a certain beggar named Lazarus, who was laid at his gate, full of sores, and desiring to be fed with the crumbs which fell from the rich man's table; moreover the dogs licked his sores."

—Luke 16:20,21

Chapter the Seventh

AS OUR SAVIOUR sat teaching the people and answering their questions, a certain lawyer stood up and said, "Master, what shall I do, that I may live again in happiness after I am dead?" Jesus said unto him, "The first of all the commandments is, the Lord our God is one Lord: and you shall love the Lord your God with all your heart, and with all your soul, and with all your mind, and with all your strength. And the second is like unto it. You shall love your neighbour as yourself. There is none other commandment greater than these!"

Then the lawyer said, "But who is my neighbour? Tell me that I may know." Jesus answered in this parable: "There was once a traveller," he said, "journeying from Jerusalem to Jericho, who fell among thieves; and they robbed him of his clothes, and wounded him, and went away, leaving him half dead upon the road. A priest, happening to pass that way, while the poor man lay there, saw him, but took no notice, and passed by on the other side. Another man, a Levite, came that way, and also saw him;

but he only looked at him for a moment, and then passed by also. But a certain Samaritan who came travelling along that road, no sooner saw him than he had compassion on him, and dressed his wounds with oil and wine, and set him on the beast he rode himself, and took him to an inn, and next morning took out of his pocket two pence and gave them to the landlord, saying, 'Take care of him and whatever you may spend beyond this, in doing so, I will repay you when I come here again.' Now which of these three men," said Our Saviour to the lawyer, "do you think should he called the neighbour of him who fell among the thieves?" The lawyer said, "The man who showed compassion on him." "True," replied Our Saviour. "Go and do likewise! Be compassionate to all men. For all men are your neighbours and brothers."

And He told them this parable, of which the meaning is, that we are never to be proud, or think ourselves very good, before God, but are always to be humble. He said, "When you are invited to a feast or wedding, do not sit down in the best place, lest some more honoured man should come, and claim that seat. But sit down in the lowest place, and a better will be offered you if you deserve it. For whosoever exalts himself shall be abased, and whosoever humbles himself shall be exalted."

He also told them this parable: "There was a certain man who prepared a great supper and invited many people, and sent his servant round to them when supper was ready to tell them they were waited for. Upon this, they made excuses. One said he had bought a piece of ground and must go to look at it. Another said that he had bought five yoke of oxen, and must go to try them. Yet another said that he was newly married and could not come. When the master of the house heard this he was angry, and told

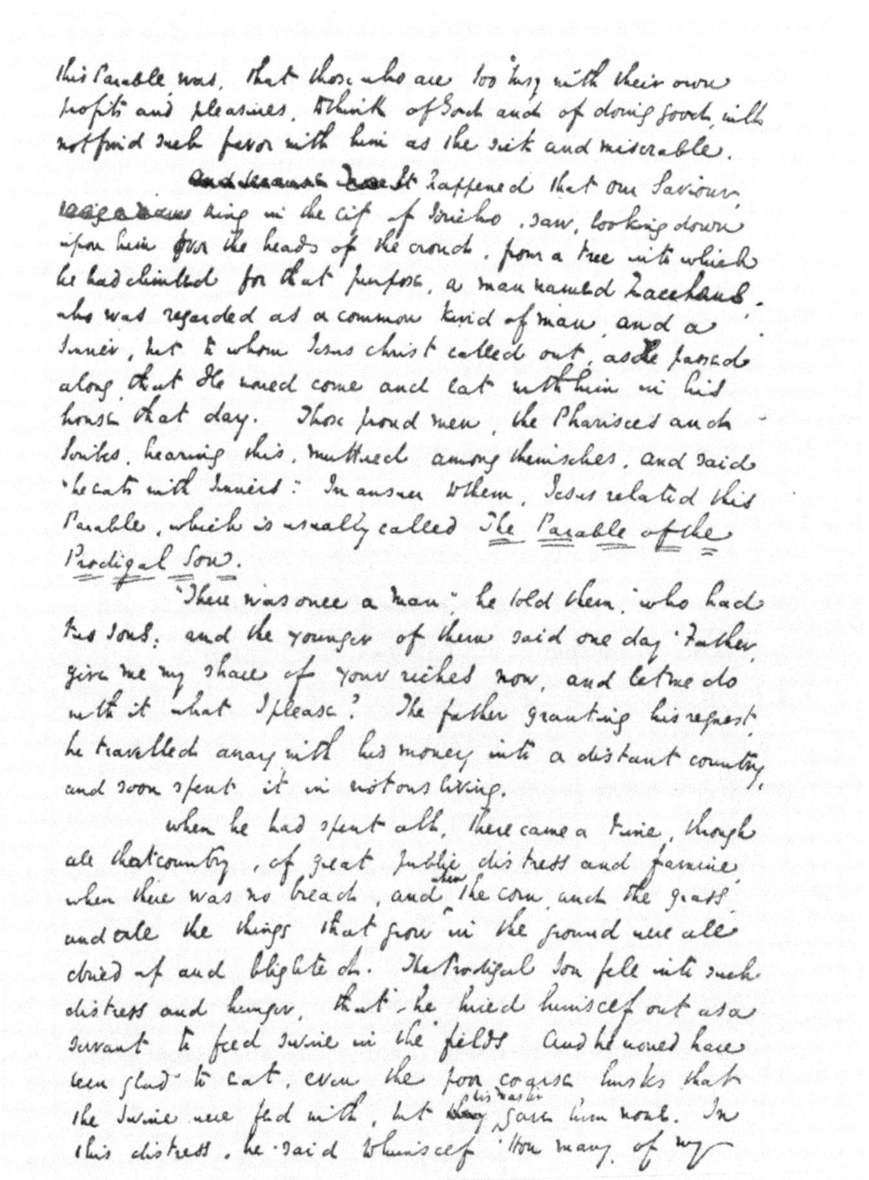

this Parable was, that those who are too busy with their own profits and pleasures, to think of God and of doing good, will not find such favor with him as the sick and miserable.

It happened that our Saviour going into the city of Jericho, saw, looking down upon him over the heads of the crowd, from a tree into which he had climbed for that purpose, a man named Zacchaeus, who was regarded as a common kind of man and a Sinner, but to whom Jesus Christ called out, as He passed along, that He would come and eat with him in his house that day. Those proud men, the Pharisees and Scribes, hearing this, muttered among themselves, and said 'He eats with Sinners.' In answer to them, Jesus related this Parable, which is usually called The Parable of the Prodigal Son.

'There was once a man,' he told them, 'who had two sons: and the younger of them said one day 'Father, give me my share of your riches now, and let me do with it what I please.' The father granting his request, he travelled away with his money into a distant country, and soon spent it in riotous living.

When he had spent all, there came a time, through all that country, of great public distress and famine, when there was no bread, and when the corn, and the grass, and all the things that grow in the ground were all dried up and blighted. The Prodigal Son fell into such distress and hunger, that he hired himself out as a servant to feed swine in the fields. And he would have been glad to eat, even the poor coarse husks that the swine were fed with, but his master gave him none. In this distress, he said to himself 'How many of my

A FACSIMILE OF A PAGE OF THE MANUSCRIPT OF CHARLES DICKENS' *LIFE OF OUR LORD.*

the servant to go into the streets, and into the high roads, and among the hedges, and invite the poor, the lame, the maimed, and the blind to supper instead."

The meaning of Our Saviour in telling them this parable, was that those who are too busy with their own profits and pleasures to think of God and of doing good, will not find such favour with Him as the sick and miserable.

It happened that Our Saviour, being in the city of Jericho, looking down upon Him over the heads of the crowd from a tree into which he had climbed for that purpose, saw a man named Zaccheus, who was regarded as a common kind of man, and a sinner, but to whom Jesus Christ called out, as He passed along, that He would come and eat with him in his house that day. Those proud men, the Pharisees and Scribes, hearing this, muttered among themselves and said, "He eats with sinners." In answer to them, Jesus related this parable, which is usually called The Parable of the Prodigal Son:

> "There was once a man," He told them, "who had two sons: and the younger of them said one day, 'Father, give me my share of your riches now, and let me do with it what I please.' The father granting his request, he travelled away with his money into a distant country, and soon spent it in riotous living.
>
> "When he had spent all, there came a time of great public distress and famine, through all that country, when there was no bread, and when the corn, and the grass, and all the things that grow in the ground were all dried up and blighted. The Prodigal Son fell into such distress and

CHAPTER THE SEVENTH

hunger that he hired himself out as a servant to feed swine in the fields. And he would have been glad to eat even the poor coarse husks that the swine were fed with, but his master gave him none. In this distress, he said to himself, 'How many of my father's servants have bread enough, and to spare, while I perish with hunger! I will arise and go to my father, and will say unto him: 'Father! I have sinned against Heaven, and before you, and am no more worthy to be called your son!'

"And so he travelled back again, in great pain and sorrow and difficulty, to his father's house. When he was yet a great way off, his father saw him, and knew him in the midst of all his rags and misery, and ran towards him and wept, and fell upon his neck and kissed him. And he told his servants to clothe this poor repentant son in the best robes, and to make a great feast to celebrate his return. This was done and they began to be merry.

"But the eldest son, who had been in the field and knew nothing of his brother's return, coming to the house and hearing the music and dancing, called to one of the servants, and asked him what it meant. To this the servant answered that his brother had come home, and that his father was joyful because of his return. At this news, the elder brother was angry and would not go into the house; so the father, hearing of it, came out to persuade him.

" 'Father,' said the elder brother, 'you do not treat me justly, to show so much joy for my younger brother's return. For these many years I have remained with you constantly, and have been true to you, yet you have never made a feast for me. But when my younger brother returns, who has been a prodigal, and riotous, and spent his money in many bad ways, you are full of delight, and the whole house makes merry!' 'Son,' returned the father, 'you have always been with me, and all I have is yours. But we thought your brother was dead, and he is alive. He was lost, and now he is found; and it is natural and right that we should be merry for his unexpected return to his old home.'"

By this, Our Saviour meant to teach that those who have done wrong and forgotten God are always welcome to Him and will always receive His mercy, if they will only return to Him in sorrow for the sin of which they have been guilty.

Now the Pharisees received these lessons from Our Saviour scornfully, for they were rich and covetous, and thought themselves superior to all mankind. As a warning to them, Christ related this parable: of Dives and Lazarus.

"There was a certain rich man who was clothed in purple and fine linen, and fared sumptuously every day. And there was a certain beggar, named Lazarus, who was laid at his gate, full of sores, and desiring to be fed with the crumbs which fell from the rich man's table. Moreover, the dogs came and licked his sores.

And it came to pass that the beggar died, and was carried by the Angels into Abraham's bosom. Abraham had been a very good man who lived many years before that time, and was then in Heaven. The rich man also died, and was buried. And in Hell, he lifted up his eyes, being in torments, and saw Abraham afar off, and Lazarus. And he cried and said, 'Father Abraham, have mercy on me, and send Lazarus that he may dip the tip of his finger in water and cool my tongue, for I am tormented in this flame.' But Abraham said, 'Son, remember that in your lifetime you received good things, and likewise Lazarus received evil things. But now he is comforted, and you are tormented!' "

Among other parables, Christ said to these same Pharisees, that because of their pride, two men once went up into the temple to pray; one was a Pharisee, and one a Publican. The Pharisee said, "God, I am thankful, that I am not unjust as other men are, or bad as this Publican is!" The Publican, standing afar off, would not lift up his eyes to Heaven, but struck his breast, and only said, "God be merciful to me, a sinner!" And God—Our Saviour told them—would be merciful to that man rather than the other, and would be better pleased with his prayer, because he made it with a humble and a lowly heart.

The Pharisees were so angry at being taught these things, that they employed some spies to ask Our Saviour questions, and tried to trap Him into saying something which was against the law. The Emperor of that country, who was called Caesar, having commanded tribute money to be regularly paid to him by the people, and being cruel against anyone who disputed his right to it, these spies thought they might, perhaps, induce Our Saviour to say it was an unjust payment, and so bring himself under the Emperor's displeasure. Therefore, pretending to be very humble, they came to Him and said, "Master, you teach the word of God rightly, and do not respect persons on account of their wealth or high station. Tell us, is it lawful that we should pay tribute to Caesar?"

Christ, who knew their thoughts, replied, "Why do you ask? Show me a penny." And they did so. "Whose image, and whose name, is this upon it?" He asked them. They said, "Caesar's." "Then," said He, "Render unto Caesar the things that are Caesar's."

So they left Him very much enraged and disappointed that they could not entrap Him. But Our Saviour knew their hearts and thoughts, as well as He knew that other men were conspiring against Him, and that He would soon be put to death.

As He was teaching them, He sat near the public treasury, where people, as they passed along the street, were accustomed to drop money into a box for the poor; and many rich persons, passing while Jesus sat there, had put in a great deal of money. At last there came a poor widow who dropped in two mites, each half a farthing in value, and then went quietly away. Jesus, seeing her do this, as He rose to leave the place called His Disciples about Him, and said to them that the poor widow had been more truly charitable than all the rest who had given great sums of money that day; for the others were rich and would never miss what they had given, but she was very poor, and had given those two mites which was all she had, and might have bought her bread to eat.

Let us never forget what the poor widow did, when we think we are charitable.

RESURRECTION OF LAZARUS

"And when He had said these things, He cried with a loud voice, 'Lazarus come forth.'"
—John 11:43

Chapter the Eighth

THERE WAS A certain man named Lazarus of Bethany, who was taken very ill; and as he was the brother of that same Mary who had anointed Christ with ointment, and wiped His feet with her hair, she and her sister Martha sent to Him, in great trouble, saying "Lord, Lazarus whom you love is sick, and likely to die."

Jesus did not go to them for two days after receiving this message; but when that time was past, He said to His Disciples, "Lazarus is dead. Let us go to Bethany." When they arrived there (it was a place very near to Jerusalem) they found, as Jesus had foretold, that Lazarus was dead, and had been dead and buried four days.

When Martha heard that Jesus was coming, she rose up from among the people who had come to console with her on her poor brother's death, and ran to meet Him, leaving her sister Mary weeping, in the house. When Martha saw Him, she burst into tears, and said, "O Lord, if You had been here, my brother would not have died." "Your brother shall rise again," returned Our Saviour. "I know he will, and I believe he will, Lord, at the

Resurrection on the Last Day," said Martha.

Jesus said to her, "I am the Resurrection and the Life. Do you believe this?" She answered, "Yes, Lord;" and running back to her sister Mary, told her that Christ had come. Mary, hearing this, ran out, followed by all those who had been grieving with her in the house, and coming to the place where He was, fell down at His feet upon the ground and wept; and so did all the rest. Jesus was so full of compassion for their sorrow that He wept too. He said, "Where have you laid him?" They said, "Lord, come and see!"

He was buried in a cave; and there was a great stone laid upon it. When they all came to the grave, Jesus ordered the stone to be rolled away, and it was done. Then, after casting up His eyes, and thanking God, He said, in a loud and solemn voice, "Lazarus, come forth!" And the dead man, Lazarus, restored to life, came out among the people, and went home with his sisters. At this sight, so awful and affecting, many of the people there believed that Jesus Christ was indeed the Son of God, who had come to instruct and save mankind. But others ran to tell the Pharisees; and from that day the Pharisees resolved among themselves that Jesus should be killed to prevent more people from believing in Him. And they agreed among themselves—meeting in the temple for that purpose—that if He came into Jerusalem before the Feast of the Passover, which was then approaching, He should be seized.

It was six days before the Passover, when Jesus raised Lazarus from the dead; and at night, when they all sat at supper together, with Lazarus among them, Mary rose up and took a pound of ointment (which was very precious and costly, and was called ointment of spikenard) and anointed the feet of Jesus Christ

CHAPTER THE EIGHTH

with it, and once again, wiped them with her hair; and the whole house was filled with the pleasant smell of the ointment. Judas Iscariot, one of the Disciples, pretended to be angry by this, and said that the ointment might have been sold for three hundred pence, and the money given to the poor. But he only said so, in reality, because he carried the purse, and was (unknown to the rest, at that time) a thief, and wished to get all the money he could. He now began to plot for betraying Christ into the hands of the chief priests.

The Feast of the Passover now drawing very near, Jesus Christ, with His Disciples, moved forward toward Jerusalem. When they were come near to that city He pointed to a village and told two of His Disciples to go there and they would find a donkey, with a colt tied to a tree, which they were to bring to Him. Finding these animals exactly as Jesus had described, they brought them to Him—and Jesus, riding on the donkey, entered Jerusalem. An immense crowd of people collected round Him as He went along the road, and throwing their robes on the ground, and cutting down green branches from the palm trees, and spreading them in His path, they shouted and cried out, "Hosanna to the Son of David!" (David had been a great King there.) "He comes in the name of the Lord! This is Jesus, the Prophet of Nazareth!" And when Jesus went into the temple, and cast out the tables of the moneychangers who wrongfully sat there, together with people who sold doves; saying, "My Father's house is a house of prayer, but you have made it a den of thieves!" When the people and children cried in the temple, "This is Jesus the Prophet of Nazareth," and would not be silenced, and when the blind and lame came flocking to Him in crowds and were healed by His hand, the chief priests, Scribes, and Pharisees were filled with fear and hatred of Him. But Jesus continued to heal the sick and do well, and went and lodged at Bethany; a place that was very near the city of Jerusalem, but not within the walls.

One night at that place, He rose from supper at which He was seated with His Disciples, and taking a cloth and a basin of water, washed their feet. Simon Peter, one of the Disciples, would have prevented Him from washing his feet, but Our Saviour told him that He did this in order that they would remember it, and always be kind and gentle to one another, knowing no pride or ill-will among themselves.

Then He became sad and grieved, and looking around on the Disciples said, "There is one here who will betray me." They cried out, one after another, "Is it I, Lord?" "Is it I?" But He only answered, "It is one of the twelve that dips with me in the dish." One of the Disciples, whom Jesus loved, happening to be leaning on His breast at that moment listening to His words, and Simon Peter beckoned to him that he should ask the name of this false man.

Jesus answered, "It is he to whom I shall give a sop when I have dipped it in the dish," and when He had dipped it, He gave it to Judas Iscariot, saying, "What you do, do quickly." The other Disciples did not understand, but Judas knew to mean that Christ had read his bad thoughts.

So Judas, taking the sop, went out immediately. It was night, and he went straight to the chief priest and said, "What will you give me if I deliver Him to you?" They agreed to give him thirty pieces of silver; and for this he undertook soon to betray into their hands his Lord and Master, Jesus Christ.

THE LAST SUPPER

"Therefore, when He had gone out, Jesus said, 'Now is the Son of Man glorified, and God is glorified in Him.'"
—John 13:31

Chapter the Ninth

THE FEAST OF the passover being almost come, Jesus said to two of His Disciples, Peter and John, "Go into the city of Jerusalem, and you will meet a man carrying a pitcher of water. Follow him home, and say to him, 'The Master says, where is the guest chamber, where He can eat the Passover with His Disciples.' And he will show you a large upper room, furnished. There make ready the supper."

The two Disciples found that it happened as Jesus had said; and having met the man with the pitcher of water, and having followed him home, and having been shown the room, they prepared the supper. Jesus and the other ten Apostles came at the usual time, and they all sat down to partake of it together.

It is always called the Last Supper, because this was the last time that Our Saviour ate and drank with His Disciples.

And He took bread from the table, and blessed it, and broke it, and gave it to them. Then He took the cup of wine, and blessed it and drank, and gave it to them, saying, "Do this in remembrance of me!" And when they had finished supper, and had sung a hymn, they went out into the Mount of Olives.

There, Jesus told them, that He would be seized that night, and that they would all leave Him alone, and would think only of their own safety. Peter earnestly said, he never would. "Before the cock crows,' returned Our Saviour, "you will deny me thrice." But Peter answered, "No, Lord. Though I should die with You, I will never deny You." And all the other Disciples said the same.

Jesus then led the way over a brook, called Cedron, into a garden that was called Gethsemane; and walked with three of the Disciples into a retired part of the garden. Then He left them as He had left the others and said, "Wait here, and watch!" He then went away and prayed by Himself, while they, being weary, fell asleep.

And Christ suffered great sorrow and distress of mind, in His prayers in that garden, because He would bear the pain of all the sins of all His people, and also because of the wickedness of the men of Jerusalem who were going to kill Him; and so He shed tears before God, and was in deep and strong affliction.

When His prayers were finished, and He was comforted, He returned to the Disciples, and said, "Rise! Let us be going! He is close at hand, who will betray me!"

Now, Judas knew that garden well, for Our Saviour had often walked there with His Disciples; and, almost at the moment when Our Saviour said these words, Judas arrived, accompanied by a strong guard of men and officers, which had been sent by the chief priests and Pharisees to arrest Jesus. It being dark, they carried lanterns and torches, and they also were armed with swords and staves, for they did not know if the people would rise

CHAPTER THE NINTH

and defend Jesus. This therefore made them afraid to seize Him boldly in the day, when He sat teaching the people.

As the leaders of this guard had never seen Jesus Christ and did not know Him from the Apostles, Judas had said to them, "The man whom I kiss will be He." As he advanced to give this wicked kiss, Jesus said to the soldiers, "Whom do you seek?" "Jesus of Nazareth," they answered. "I am He," said Our Saviour, "Let my Disciples here go freely. I am He." Which Judas confirmed, by saying, "Hail Master!" and kissed Him. Whereupon Jesus said, "Judas, you betray me with a kiss!"

The guard then ran forward to seize Him. No one offered to protect Him, except Peter, who drew his sword, and cut off the right ear of the high priest's servant, who was with the soldiers, and whose name was Malchus. But Jesus made him sheathe his sword, and gave Himself up. Then, all the Disciples forsook Him and fled; and there remained not one—not one—to bear Him company.

THE CRUCIFIXION OF CHRIST

"He said, 'It is finished!' And bowing his head,
He gave up His spirit."
—John 19:30

Chapter the Tenth

AFTER A SHORT time, peter and another disciple took heart, and secretly followed the guard to the house of Caiaphas the high priest, to find where Jesus was taken and where the Scribes and others were assembled to question Him. Peter stood at the door, but the other Disciple, who was known to the high priest, went in and presently returning, asked the woman, who kept the door, to admit Peter too. She, looking at him, said, "Are you not one of the Disciples?" He said, "I am not." So she let him in and he stood before a fire that was there, warming himself along with the servants and officers who were crowded round it. For it was very cold.

Some of these men asked him the same question as the woman had done and said, "Are you not one of the Disciples?" He again denied it, and said, "I am not." One of them, who was related to that man whose ear Peter had cut off with his sword said, "Did I not see you in the garden with Him?" Peter again denied it with an oath and said, "I do not know the man." Immediately the cock

THE LIFE OF OUR LORD

crowed, and Jesus, turning round, looked steadfastly at Peter. Then Peter remembered what He had said, that before the cock crowed, he would deny Him three times—and he went out and wept bitterly.

Among other questions that were put to Jesus, the high priest asked Him what He had taught the people. To which He answered that He had taught them in the open day, and in the open streets, and that the priests should ask the people what they had learned from Him. One of the officers struck Jesus with his hand for this reply; and two false witnesses coming in, said they had heard Him say that He could destroy the Temple of

God and build it again in three days. Jesus answered little, but the Scribes and priests agreed that He was guilty of blasphemy, and should be put to death. Then they spat upon and beat Him.

When Judas Iscariot saw that his Master was indeed condemned, he was so full of horror for what he had done, that he took the thirty pieces of silver back to the chief priests, and said, "I have betrayed innocent blood! I cannot keep it!" With those words, he threw the money down upon the floor, and rushing away, wild with despair, hanged himself. The rope was weak and broke with the weight of his body, after he had died, and he fell down on the ground, all bruised and burst—a dreadful sight to see!

The chief priests, not knowing what else to do with the thirty pieces of silver, bought a burying-place for strangers with it, the proper name of which was the Potters' Field. But the people called it the Field of Blood, ever afterwards.

Jesus was taken from the high priests to the judgment hall where Pontius Pilate, the Governor sat to administer justice.

CHAPTER THE TENTH

Pilate (who was not a Jew) said to Him: "Your own people, the Jews, and your own priests have delivered you to me. What have you done?"

Finding that He had done no harm, Pilate went out and told the Jews so; but they said, "He has been teaching the people what is not true, and what is wrong; and He began to do so, long ago, in Galilee," As Herod had the right to punish people who offended against the law in Galilee, Pilate said, "I find no wrong in Him. Let Him be taken before Herod!"

They carried Jesus accordingly before Herod, where he sat surrounded by his stern soldiers and men in armour. And these laughed at Jesus, and dressed him in mockery, in a fine robe, and sent Him back to Pilate. And Pilate called the priests and people together again and said, "I find no wrong in this man, neither does Herod. He has done nothing to deserve death." But they cried out, "He has, He has! Yes, yes! Let Him be killed!"

Pilate was troubled in his mind to hear them so clamorous against Jesus Christ. His wife, too, had dreamed all night about it, and sent to him upon the judgment seat, saying, "Have nothing to do with that just man!" As it was the custom at the Feast of the Passover to give some prisoner his liberty, Pilate endeavoured to persuade the people to ask for the release of Jesus. But they said (being very ignorant and passionate, and being told to do so, by the priests), "No, no, we will not have Him released. Release Barabbas, and let this man be crucified!"

Barabbas was a wicked criminal, in jail for his crimes, and in danger of being put to death. Pilate, finding the people so determined against Jesus, delivered Him to the soldiers to be scourged (that is beaten). They plaited a crown of thorns, and put it on His head, and dressed Him in a purple robe, and spat upon Him, and struck Him with their hands, and said, "Hail, King of the Jews!" remembering that the crowd had called Him the Son of David when He entered into Jerusalem. And they ill-used Him in many cruel ways; but Jesus bore it patiently, and only said, "Father! Forgive them! They know not what they do!"

Once more, Pilate brought Him out before the people, dressed in the purple robe and crown of thorns, and said, "Behold the man!" They cried out, savagely, "Crucify Him! Crucify Him!" So did the chief priests and officers. "Take Him and crucify Him yourselves," said Pilate. "I find no fault in Him." But they cried out, He called Himself the Son of God; and that, by the Jewish law, is deserving of death! And He called himself King of the Jews; and that is against the Roman law, for we have no King but Caesar, the Roman Emperor. If you let Him go, you are not Caesar's friend. Crucify Him! Crucify Him!"

When Pilate saw that he could not prevail with them, however hard he tried, he called for water, and washing his hands before the crowd, said, "I am innocent of the blood of this just man." Then he delivered Jesus to them to be crucified; and shouting and gathering round Him, and treating Him (who still prayed for them to God) with cruelty and insult, they took Him away.

THE RESURRECTION

*"And the angel answered and said unto the women,
Fear not: for I know that you seek Jesus, who was crucified.
He is not here, for He is risen, as He said.
Come see the place where the Lord lay."*
—Matthew 28:5,6

Chapter the Eleventh

THAT YOU MAY know what the people meant when they said, "Crucify Him!" I must tell you that in those times, which were very cruel times indeed (let us thank God and Jesus Christ that they are past!), it was the custom to kill people who were sentenced to death, by nailing them alive on a great wooden cross, planted upright in the ground, and leaving them there, exposed to the sun and wind, day and night, until they died of pain and thirst. It was the custom as well to make them walk to the place of execution, carrying the cross-piece of wood to which their hands were to be afterwards nailed, that their shame and suffering might be the greater.

Bearing His cross upon His shoulder, like the commonest and most wicked criminal, Our Blessed Saviour, Jesus Christ, surrounded by the persecuting crowd, went out of Jerusalem to a place called, in the Hebrew language, Golgotha; that is, the place of the Skulls. And coming to a hill called Mount Calvary, they hammered cruel nails through His hands and feet, and nailed

Him on the cross, between two other crosses, on each of which a common thief was nailed in agony.

Over His head they fastened this writing: "Jesus of Nazareth, the King of the Jews" in three languages: in Hebrew, in Greek, and in Latin.

In the meantime, a guard of four soldiers sitting on the ground divided His clothes (which they had taken off) into four parcels for themselves, and cast lots for His coat, and sat there, gambling and talking, while He suffered. They offered Him vinegar to drink, mixed with gall; and wine, mixed with myrrh; but He took none. And the wicked people who passed that way mocked Him, and said, "If You are the Son of God, come down from the cross." The chief priests also mocked Him, and said, "He came to save sinners. Let Him save Himself!" One of the thieves, too, railed at Him, in His torture, and said, "If You are Christ, save Yourself, and us." But the other thief, who was penitent, said, "Lord! Remember me when You come into Your Kingdom!" And Jesus answered, "Today you will be with me in Paradise."

There were none to take pity on Him, but one Disciple and four women. God blessed those women for their true and tender hearts! They were the mother of Jesus, His mother's sister, Mary, the wife of Cleophas, and Mary Magdalene who had twice dried His feet upon her hair. The Disciple was he whom Jesus loved, John, who had leaned upon His breast and asked Him which was the betrayer. When Jesus saw them standing at the foot of the cross He said to His mother that John would be her son, to comfort her when He was dead; and from that hour John was as a son to her, and loved her.

CHAPTER THE ELEVENTH

At about the sixth hour, a deep and terrible darkness came over all the land, and lasted until the ninth hour, when Jesus cried out, with a loud voice, "My God, my God, why have You forsaken me!" The soldiers, hearing Him, dipped a sponge in some vinegar that was standing there, and fastening it to a long reed, put it up to His mouth. When He had received it, He said, "It is finished!" And crying, "Father! Into Your hands I commend my spirit!" He died.

Then there was a dreadful earthquake, and the great veil of the temple was torn from top to bottom. The guards, terrified at these sights, said to each other, "Surely this was the Son of God!" The people who had been watching the cross from a distance (among whom were many women) smote upon their breasts, and went home fearful and sad.

The next day, being the Sabbath, the Jews were anxious that the condemned on crosses should be taken down at once, and made that request to Pilate. Therefore some soldiers came and broke the legs of the two criminals to kill them, but coming to Jesus, and finding Him already dead, they only pierced His side with a spear. From the wound there came out blood and water.

There was a good man named Joseph of Arimathea—a Jewish city—who believed in Christ, and going to Pilate privately (for fear of the Jews) begged that he might be given the body. Pilate consenting, he and another Jewish leader, Nicodemus, rolled it in linen and spices—which was the custom of the Jews to prepare bodies for burial in that way and buried it in a new tomb or sepulchre, which had been cut out of a rock in a garden near to the place of crucifixion, and where no one had ever yet been buried. They then rolled a great stone to the mouth of the

THE LIFE OF OUR LORD

sepulchre, and left Mary Magdalene, and the other Mary, sitting there, watching it.

The chief priests and Pharisees, remembering that Jesus Christ had said to His Disciples that He would rise from the grave on the third day after His death, went to Pilate and prayed that the sepulchre might be watched over until that day, lest the Disciples should steal the body, and afterwards say to the people that Christ was risen from the dead. Pilate agreeing to this, a guard of soldiers was set over it constantly, and the stone was also sealed up. And so it remained, watched and sealed, until the third day, which was the first day of the week.

When that morning began to dawn, Mary Magdalene and the other Mary and some other women, came to the sepulchre, with some more spices, which they had prepared. As they were saying to each other, "How shall we roll away the stone?" the earth trembled and shook, and an Angel, descending from Heaven, rolled it back, and then sat resting on it. His countenance was like lightning, and his garments were white as snow; and at sight of him the men of the guard fainted away with fear, as if they were dead.

Mary Magdalene saw the stone rolled away, and waiting to see no more, ran to Peter and John who were coming towards the place, and said, "They have taken away the Lord and we know not where they have laid Him!" They immediately ran to the tomb, but John, being the faster of the two, outran the other and got there first. He stooped down and looked in, and saw the linen clothes in which the body had been wrapped, lying there; but he did not go in. "When Peter came up, he went in, and saw the linen clothes lying in one place, and a napkin that had been bound about the head, in another. John also went in then, and

CHAPTER THE ELEVENTH

saw the same things. Then they went home to tell the rest.

But Mary Magdalene remained outside the sepulchre, weeping. After a little time she stooped down and looked in and saw two Angels, clothed in white, sitting where the body of Christ had lain. These said to her, "Woman, why are you weeping?" She answered, "Because they have taken away my Lord, and I know not where they have laid Him." As she gave this answer, she turned round and saw Jesus standing behind her, but did not know it was Him. "Woman," He said, "why are you weeping? What are you seeking?" She, supposing Him to be the gardener, replied, "Sir! If You have taken my Lord, tell me where you have laid Him, and I will take Him away!"

Jesus then said to her, "Mary." Then she knew Him and exclaimed, "Master!"—"Do not touch me," said Christ; "for I am not yet ascended to my Father; but go to my Disciples and say unto them, I ascend unto my Father, and your Father; and to my God, and to your God!"

Accordingly, Mary Magdalene went and told the Disciples that she had seen Christ, and what He had said to her; and with them she found the other women whom she had left at the sepulchre when she had gone to call the two Disciples, Peter and John. These women told her and the rest that they had seen at the tomb two men in shining garments, at sight of whom they had been afraid, and had stooped down, but who had told them that the Lord was risen; and also that as they came to tell us they had seen Christ on the way, and had held Him by the feet and worshipped Him. But these accounts seemed to the Apostles, at that time, as idle tales, and they did not believe them.

The soldiers of the guard too, when they recovered from

their fainting-fit, they went to the chief priests to tell them what they had seen. They were immediately bribed and silenced with large sums of money, and were told to say that the Disciples had stolen the body away while they were asleep.

But it happened that on that same day, Simon and Cleopas—Simon one of the twelve Apostles, and Cleopas one of the followers of Christ—were walking to a village called Emmaus, at some little distance from Jerusalem, and were talking by the way, upon the death and resurrection of Christ, when they were joined by a stranger who explained the Scriptures to them, and told them a great deal about God, so that they wondered at His knowledge. As the night was fast coming on when they reached the village, they asked this stranger to stay with them, which He consented to do. When they all three sat down to supper, He took some bread, and blessed it, and broke it as Christ had done at the Last Supper. Looking on Him in wonder they found that His face changed before them, and that it was Christ Himself; and as they looked on Him, He disappeared.

They instantly rose up and returned to Jerusalem, and finding the Disciples sitting together, told them what they had seen. While they were speaking, Jesus suddenly stood in the midst of all the company, and said, "Peace be unto you!" Seeing that they were greatly frightened, He showed them His hands and feet, and invited them to touch Him; and to encourage them and give them time to recover themselves, He ate a piece of broiled fish and a piece of honeycomb before them all.

But Thomas, one of the twelve Apostles, was not there at that time; and when the rest said to him afterwards, "We have seen the Lord!" he answered, "Except I shall see in His hands the print

CHAPTER THE ELEVENTH

of the nails, and thrust my hand into His side, I will not believe!" At that moment, though the doors were all shut, Jesus again appeared, standing among them, and said, "Peace be unto you!" Then He said to Thomas, "Reach your finger here, and behold my hands; and reach your hand, and thrust it into my side; and be not faithless, but believing." And Thomas answered, and said to Him, "My Lord and my God!" Then said Jesus, "Thomas, because you have seen me, you have believed. Blessed are they that have not seen me, and yet have believed."

After that time, Jesus Christ was seen by five hundred of His followers at once, and He remained with others of them forty days, teaching them and instructing them to go forth into the world, and preach His gospel and religion: not minding what wicked men might do to them. And conducting His Disciples at last out of Jerusalem as far as Bethany, He blessed them, and ascended in a cloud to Heaven, and took His place at the right hand of God.

And while they gazed into the bright blue sky where He had vanished, two white-robed Angels appeared among them, and told them that as they had seen Christ ascend to Heaven, so He would, one day, come descending from it to judge the world.

When Christ was seen no more, the Apostles began to teach the people as He had commanded them. And having chosen a new apostle, named Matthias, to replace the wicked Judas, they wandered into all countries, telling the people of Christ's life and death and of His Crucifixion and Resurrection and of the lessons he had taught and baptizing them in Christ's name. And through the power He had given them they healed the sick, and gave sight to the blind, and speech to the dumb, and hearing to the deaf, as

103

THE LIFE OF OUR LORD

THE ASCENSION

"And it came to pass, while He blessed them, He was parted from them and carried up into heaven."
—Luke 24:51

CHAPTER THE ELEVENTH

He had done. And Peter, having been thrown into prison, was delivered from his chains, in the dead of night, by an Angel. And once, his words before God caused a man named Ananias, and his wife Sapphira, who had told a lie, to be struck down dead, upon the earth.

Wherever the Apostles went, they were persecuted and cruelly treated. One man named Saul, who had held the clothes of some barbarous persons, who pelted one of the Christians, named Stephen, to death with stones, was always active in doing them harm. But God turned Saul's heart afterwards; for as he was travelling to Damascus to search out some Christians who were there, and drag them to prison, there shone about him a great light from Heaven, and a voice cried, "Saul, Saul, why do you persecute me!" and he was struck down from his horse by an invisible hand in sight of all the guards and soldiers who were riding with him. When they raised him, they found that he was blind; and so he remained for three days, neither eating nor drinking, until one of the Christians (sent to him by an Angel for that purpose) restored his sight in the name of Jesus Christ.

Afterwards he became a Christian, and preached, and taught, and believed, with the Apostles, and did great works in Jesus' name. They took the name of Christians from Our Saviour Christ, and carried crosses as their sign, because upon a cross He had suffered death. The religions that were then in the world were false and brutal, and encouraged men to violence. Beasts, and even men, were killed in the churches, in the belief that the pouring out of their blood was pleasant to the gods—there were supposed to be a great many gods and many most cruel and disgusting ceremonies prevailed. Yet, for all this, and though the Christian religion was such a true, and kind, and good one, the priests of the old religions long persuaded the people to do all possible injury to the Christians. As a result many of the Christians were hanged, beheaded, burnt, buried alive, and devoured in theatres by wild beasts for the public amusement, during many years.

Nothing would silence them or terrify them though, for they knew that if they did obeyed and held fast, they would go to Heaven. So thousands upon thousands of Christians sprung up and taught the people and were cruelly killed, and were succeeded by other Christians, until the religion gradually became the greatest religion of the world.

Remember! It is Christianity TO DO GOOD, always!—even to those who do evil to us. It is Christianity to love our neighbours as ourself, and to do to others as we would have them do to us. It is Christianity to be gentle, merciful, and forgiving, and to keep those qualities quiet in our own hearts, and never make a boast of them, or of our prayers or of our love of God, but always to show that we love Him by humbly trying to do right in everything. If we do this, and remember the life and lessons of Our Lord Jesus Christ, and try to act up to them, we may confidently hope that God will forgive us our sins and mistakes, and enable us to live and die in peace.

CHAPTER THE ELEVENTH

drinking, until one of the Christians (sent by God an angel for that purpose) restored his sight in the name of Jesus Christ. After which he became a Christian, and preached, and taught, and lived, with the apostles, and did great service.

They took the name of Christians from Our Saviour Christ, and carried crosses as their sign, because upon a Cross He had suffered Death. The Religions that were then in the world were false and brutal, and encouraged men to violence Beasts, and even men were killed in the churches, under the idea, that the smell of their blood was pleasant to the Gods — there were supposed to be a great many Gods — and many cruel and disgusting ceremonies prevailed. Yet for all this, and though the Christian Religion was such a true, and kind, and good one, the Priests of the old Religions so long persuaded the people to do all possible hurt to the Christians; and Christians were hanged, beheaded, burnt, buried alive, and devoured in Theatres by Wild Beasts for the public amusement, during many years. Nothing would silence them, or terrify them though; for they knew that if they did this duty they would go to Heaven. So thousands upon thousands of Christians sprung up and taught the people and were cruelly killed and were succeeded by other Christians, until the Religion gradually became the great religion of the world.

Remember! It is Christianity to do good always — even to those who do evil to us. It is Christianity to love our neighbour as ourselves, and to do to all men as we would have them Do to us. It is Christianity to be gentle, merciful, and forgiving, and to keep those qualities quiet in our own hearts, and never make a boast of them, or of our prayers, or of our love of God, but always to shew that we love Him by humbly trying to do right in everything. If we do this, and remember the life and lessons of Our Lord Jesus Christ, and try to act up to them, we may confidently hope that God will forgive us our sins and mistakes, and enable us to live and die in Peace.

A FACSIMILE OF THE LAST PAGE OF THE MANUSCRIPT OF CHARLES DICKENS' LIFE OF OUR LORD.

TWO PRAYERS WRITTEN BY CHARLES DICKENS FOR HIS YOUNG CHILDREN

Hear what our Lord Jesus christ taught to His Disciples and to us, and what we should remember every day of our lives, to love the Lord our God with all our heart, and with all our mind, and with all our soul, and with all our strength; to love our neighbours as ourselves, to do unto other people as we would have them do unto us and to be charitable and gentle to all.

There is no other commandment, our Lord Jesus Christ said, greater than these.

FOR THE EVENING

O God, who has made everything, and is so kind and merciful to everything He has made, who is all good and deserves our praise; God bless my dear Papa and Mamma, Brothers and Sisters and all my Relations and Friends. Make me a good little child, and let me never be naughty and tell a lie, which is a mean and shameful thing. Make me kind to my nurses and servants, and to all beggars and poor people, and let me never be cruel to any creatures, for if I am cruel to anything, even to a poor little fly, God, who is so good, will not be happy. And pray God to bless and preserve us all, this night, and forevermore, through Jesus Christ our Lord. Amen.

EDITOR BIOGRAPHY

Gene Fedele has been writing and editing Christian books for nearly 20 years. His most popular work is *Heroes of the Faith* (Bridge-Logos, 2003)—a collection of mini-biographies of 70 eminent men and women who have changed the course of humanity through their resolute faith and devotion to Jesus Christ. *Heroes of the Faith* is now in its fifth edition, and has been published in several languages including Chinese Mandarin and Romanian.

Fedele has been author and editor of more than a dozen books including several that are part of Bridge-Logos' Pure Gold Classics collection:

- *Pilgrim's Progress, In Words of One-Syllable*
  (Christian Family Publications, 1998; Bridge-Logos, 2003)
- *Great Christian Biographies*
  (Christian Family Publications, 1999-2001)
- *Golden Thoughts of Mother, Home & Heaven*
  (Bridge-Logos, 2003)

- *Secret Power*, by D. L. Moody
  (Pure Gold Classics, Bridge-Logos, 2006)
- *The Overcoming Life*, by D. L. Moody
  (Pure Gold Classics, Bridge-Logos, 2007)
- *Walking With God*, by Andrew Murray
  (Pure Gold Classics, Bridge-Logos, 2008)

Fedele was also founder, contributor, and editor of the *Christian Family Journal* from 1998-2005, with global distribution to more than 20 countries on 5 continents.

In addition to his literary work, Fedele has been a leader in corporate media, marketing and publishing for nearly 40 years and been honored with more that 200 awards for his creative marketing and publishing work. He has also been instrumental in planting churches in the U.S. and serving on Christian boards, including Life For The World, an orphanage and school in Haiti. He currently manages a business growth and marketing consulting firm he founded in 2014 in St. Augustine, FL, where he resides with his wife, Kerri, of 35 years, along with his three daughters and four grand-daughters.

ALSO AVAILABLE FROM BRIDGE-LOGOS

HEROES OF THE FAITH
Gene Fedele

Inspiring stories and compelling biographical sketches of 70 heroes of the faith, spanning 2000 years, who championed the cause of Christianity regardless of the obstacles.

Read about those both past and present who have carried forth the Gospel in powerful ways, demonstrating what the grace of God can do with humble men and women of all ages who choose to do His will. Let their stories inspire and encourage you to hear what God wants you to do and to step forth knowing that the same grace that was with them will be with you.

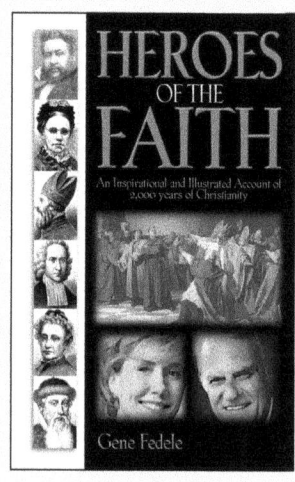

Facebook.com/genefedele
openboxcreativesolutions.com
amazon.com/author/genefedele

ISBN: 978-0-88270-934-5

www.ingramcontent.com/pod-product-compliance
Ingram Content Group UK Ltd.
Pitfield, Milton Keynes, MK11 3LW, UK
UKHW021303180426
11947UKWH00015B/993